NORTH COUNTRY TAPESTRY

Sylvia Mary McCosh 1988

NORTH COUNTRY TAPESTRY

Written for the love of our land
and all that lives therein

by

Sylvia Mary McCosh

DALEMAIN   PENRITH   CUMBRIA
HUNTIFELD   BIGGAR   SCOTLAND
1991

By the same author:

Between Two Gardens, published 1982

ISBN 0 9518690 0 0

Obtainable from
Dalemain Estates, Penrith, Cumbria CA11 0HB

Printed by Titus Wilson & Son Kendal, Cumbria

Sylvia Mary McCosh died on 17th August 1991.

This book is published posthumously by her family.

ACKNOWLEDGEMENTS

My thanks are due to Mrs. Pat Dunbar for all the trouble she has taken in typing my manuscripts and for her helpful advice. Also to my cousin Nielly Bathurst for allowing me to use her photographs including the one on the front cover. The rest of the colour photographs were taken by members of the family.

To Rosemary Verey for writing the foreword with such warmth and so much understanding of what I have tried to express. Her praise is much too generous, making me feel very humble.

To John Hurst, Editor of our splendid Cumberland and Westmorland Herald, who with his predecessor, Frank Shaw, encouraged me to bring this book together.

The frontispiece photograph of Sylvia Mary McCosh is reproduced by kind permission of Michael Arron of Hale, Cheshire.

CONTENTS

Part I
THE TURNING YEAR

Part II
EARLY SUMMER'S MAGIC

Part III
AUTUMN'S FULFILMENT

Part IV
LATER MONTHS

ILLUSTRATIONS

THE REASON WHY

The gardening, countryside articles in this book have been written for *The Cumberland and Westmorland Herald* over a period since early 1984, which this excellent local newspaper, covering a wide area, has been kind enough to publish once a month. It has given me very great pleasure to write many thoughts, sometimes relating to my family and our homes, the woods, and fields, the birds and little creatures that live therein.

In addition, I hope that my love of poetry will bring much pleasure to you as readers of my North Country way of life.

AS REFRESHING AS COOL COUNTRY AIR . . .

Although weekly newspapers are essentially about news, pictures and advertisements, some of the most popular pages are those devoted to reminiscent nostalgia and to personal memories and thoughts on a vast range of personal interests and leisure pursuits.

For many years page eight of the Penrith-based *Cumberland and Westmorland Herald* has featured many such articles — pipe-smoking Frank Alcock on walking the hills of the Lake District, George Bott on the history and personalities of Keswick, Clare Hallam on aspects of the life and traditions of the Upper Eden Valley and Jack Varty ("Mr Penrith") on memories of the town of his boyhood.

Prominent among our many valued contributors to page eight is Sylvia Mary McCosh, Cumbria's lady of the flowers. Her monthly articles on her gardens at Dalemain, on the fringe of the Lakes, and Huntfield, in the South of Scotland, bring into our living rooms a refreshing breath of cool country air, delicately scented with the fragrance of roses after rain, a hint of ripening Victoria plums, the delicacy of snowdrop-covered banks, the crisp tang of newly-mown grass and the rare delights of Dalemain's Wild Garden.

Her writings inspire placid pictures of rich colour and delectable vistas. They spread some of Sylvia's knowledge and bubbling enthusiasm to many thousands of fellow gardeners and bring smiles of pleasure and contentment to the less energetic.

Though *Herald* readers have savoured these monthly articles over the past decade or so, they are worthy of a far wider readership. In a helter-skelter world, fraught with all kinds of problems and anxieties, a source of quiet relaxation is an hour or so with Sylvia Mary McCosh, possibly as she tends the tea roses, browses over the Wendy House of her childhood days in the Dalemain garden or goes about one of the hundreds of chores which are a bore to some but a delight to this writer and her many followers.

Old-style values underly her writings. Technology and big city whizkids no doubt make some contribution to life in the 1990s but true beauty and inner satisfaction in a garden still depend on the qualities of personal endeavour — planting, tending, caring.

Love, devotion and commitment are vital factors and you will find them all in the pages of this fine book.

Penrith.
July 1991

John Hurst
(Editor, Cumberland and Westmorland Herald)

FOREWORD

This book is a true mirror of Sylvia McCosh's whole life. Born and brought up at Dalemain, an estate steeped in history, her love of her home, her garden and the surrounding countryside shines through these pages. Carrying on the tradition of her ancestors, she is the essence of William Lawson's 17th-century Country House-Wife — practical, deeply rooted in the soil and aware of the beauty and continuity of nature, the light in all its moods, the seasons and festivals as they come and pass. She has eyes for every present-day detail and emotive memories of her childhood as she gardened with Will Stuart, who worked at Dalemain for fifty-three years.

"What was Paradise?", wrote William Lawson, "but a Garden, an Orchard of Trees and Herbs, full of pleasure, and nothing there but delights." Sylvia McCosh is intuitively aware of this and *North Country Tapestry*, originally written as articles for *The Cumberland and Westmorland Herald*, reveal her feelings as well as her knowledge. All this has been gathered through her lifelong contact with the land and the countrymen who worked on her estate, her understanding of garden history and, perhaps most importantly, her love of horticulture. It is wonderful that Sylvia has found time to write and so share so many of her thoughts, and this record of her all-embracing love of nature and her family home is a priceless inheritance for her grandchildren, whom she has watched grow and flourish as she has watched the plants in her garden develop from seed to fruition.

This book should become a 20th-century classic — an inspiration for gardeners and those who cherish our countryside.

Rosemary Verey

Dalemain

COUNTRY CHILDHOOD

Memory is a treasured art
Where times and customs change and pass
Where sounds and vision play their part
As autumn turns the flowering grass —
    Turns the fresh qualities of spring
    And in its stead some newer thing.

And so for little ones ahead,
My pen is urged to write, that they
May know the happy life I led
The simple things, a country way.
    When horses pulled the farmer's cart
    And gigs and dog-carts played their part.

A motor car was seldom used
Nor aeroplanes for summer jaunts;
Electric lights switched out at ten
While flower filled fields our summer haunts
    No television whiled the hours
    Sweet meadows filled with hay and flowers.

For I was reared a country child,
With ponies, walked the furthest way
The secret reaches of the fells
Where skylarks soared; those peaceful days.
    Why do you leave the land you love
    My father often said, I trove.

Our country customs changed with time
With yet another war to save
Our land, our freedom, all at stake
We fought and beat that fearsome knave
    While we, in turn, have grown with time
    Life ceased to be our world sublime.

AND NOW THERE ARE TWO

It is a somewhat unusual challenge to work and care for two gardens, situated almost a hundred miles apart on either side of the Debatable Lands in the Border country; it certainly is an exciting challenge, but one which of necessity we undertake. Regularly all the year round, my husband Bryce and I travel between Dalemain, where I was born and brought up, and Huntfield, our Scottish home where we have lived for most of our married life.

Huntfield is a comfortable old house sheltered by numerous fine trees which lend dignity and give very necessary shelter, for our home was built a thousand feet above sea level among peaceful heather-clad hills not far from the small market town of Biggar where Lanarkshire and Peeblesshire meet across the Biggar Water.

The Clyde flows on the westerly side of Huntfield Hill, meandering on its long journey through Lanark's fertile valley till it meets with the sea beyond the busy Port of Glasgow. On the other side of our Huntfield Hill crystal burns chatter and flow in easterly and southerly directions until they join the great river Tweed as it flows its many miles to meet the North Sea.

It was here that our three sons were brought up as country children, rode their ponies, built little houses, bred bantams, guinea fowl and ornamental duck until foxes killed the latter when they escaped from their allotted pools and runs. There is always water, even in the driest weather, and here in wonderful acid soil I can garden to my heart's content. Wind was, and always will be, our worst enemy, combined with long winters, but snow, of more than ample proportions, covers and protects our treasures from ravages of winter.

In 1972 my father died at Dalemain and we were left with the burden of death duties, and also much necessary repair work, to be gradually undertaken. There was much to be done in order to make part of the house habitable, and later, another part, including The Brew House for Robert and his bride when they married in 1980.

We had to plan for the future preservation of Dalemain, while we are its "caretakers"; and for the fields, the fells and the waters of the estate. The house must be opened to visitors and the gardens likewise. There is so much to see, so much to be enjoyed by the many travellers who visit Cumbria and the Lake District. After all, it is nothing new to welcome strangers to one's home. In long ago days, travellers were given much needed hospitality: they brought news of the outside world, and were seldom turned away.

On Easter Day 1977 our first visitors arrived in the cobbled courtyard enclosed by ancient stone buildings with haylofts, stables and workshops, past the garden centre and our shop set up in the cart horse stable with its former hayloft and thence to the front door of the early Georgian house. House guides are ready to answer the visitors many questions. "Do the family really use these rooms?" is often asked and the guides delight in telling them about family parties in these beautiful rooms warmed by every blink of sunlight. Parties for our grandchildren too, with log fires burning cheerfully in the Georgian grates. Not only portraits of ancestors look down to watch the fun, for amongst them are portraits of some of our own family and their children. An old house must keep up to date with present years to remain "alive".

Dalemain

Springtime at Huntfield

Winter . . . and Springtime, Huntfield

Into the Georgian dining room our visitors move where the portrait of my great-grandfather hangs. An able barrister, he left the estate, its farms and our home in good order, and in addition doing untold good beyond. He became the first chairman of the Lancaster-Carlisle railway, and it was through his ability and persuasive powers that many reluctant land owners and farmers agreed to this new invention passing across their land. Talking to such people entailed riding for many miles in all weathers.

Portraits of some of my own fell ponies also hang in the dining room. Their pictures give me so much pleasure, painted by our old friend, the Scottish artist, Norman Miller-Miller, who also painted portraits of many of our family.

On into the medieval pele tower, now the home of the Westmorland & Cumberland Yeomanry museums. Then up the spiral stone staircase and into panelled rooms above the hall of the earlier part of the house. Down Sir Edward Hasell's new staircase designed by James Swingler, the seventeenth century builder, in 1684. Here a tiny red door with brass knocker built in one of the risers is the home of Mrs Mouse and her family. Children and their parents are often to be seen on their knees, peering through a window into Mrs Mouse's comfortable kitchen.

Our visitors are usually ready for home-made lunch or tea after seeing so many interesting and treasured things on their tour. Meals are served in the Old Hall, where a huge log fire burns in the wide arched fireplace, always welcome on a cold day.

At last, out into the garden which has grown from a herb and vegetable garden necessary to support families who lived and worked in and around the medieval tower house in long ago centuries. As the years went past, unusual trees, lawns and flowers embellished the buildings. Fragrant China roses, some a hundred years old, grow around windows on either side of the front door which visitors pass on their way to the Terrace. Rambling roses in variety grow all along this gravelled walk draping the ha-ha above the eighteenth century Low Garden: they also adorn James Swingler's enormously high wall behind the long herbaceous border. This wall, built as a feature, gives protection and warmth: in addition it shelters the courtyard behind the wall.

At the furthest end of the Terrace, Sir Edward planted a Grecian silver fir: now it is possibly the oldest and has the largest girth in Britain. This tree shelters the Knot Garden, fragrant with dwarf boxwood hedging round small shaped beds filled with herbs and low growing flowers. A Roman fountain is the centrepiece of this garden: it is a paradise for birds to wash and preen themselves in its spray.

Wander up into the High Garden, where many old varieties of apples grow amongst shrub and species roses. The sixteenth-century gazebo and the early eighteenth-century summerhouse are built against the top wall. The view of the garden with the house and courtyard barns is really beautiful from this point. A door in the wall passes into Lob's Wood, with its peaceful path above the Dacre Beck which flows beneath a steep bank, past the Wild Garden. A stone staircase leads into this tranquil garden, planted with flowering shrubs, apple trees, bulbs, blue poppies and wild flowers.

Return along the Terrace and past the front door to the little wooded Grove beyond the house. Carpets of aconites and snowdrops are glorious in springtime, later becoming a lovely place to wander on a summer's day.

After gardening for as many hours as possible and caring for all my plants, we travel back to Huntfield to start all over again.

This garden is open too, but only on special occasions in aid of charities under Scotland's Gardens Scheme, and other charities including Meningitis Research, St Columba's Hospice, and local charities. Sometimes specially arranged bus parties arrive to see the garden and I give them home-made teas, which are very popular events, especially with American visitors.

Here *Meconopsis grandis* and its variations multiply and flourish: primulas of many species and varieties also: the soil is ideal for their growth, while snow, frequently lying late, makes them feel at home, so many originating from the Sino-Himalayas. The soil is suited to azaleas and their like, but the garden is at too high an altitude for their comfort.

Herbaceous plants increase easily: strangers often remark on their height compared to those growing further south in drier areas. But, and there is a great but, spring comes late and frosts are liable to come early. Plant life is all too quickly ready to go to bed.

Only the trees, and there are many beautiful old trees, remain to clothe our peaceful acres. Migrating birds come from the North and from Scandinavian winter, bringing endless pleasure when they call to let us know that they have arrived once more.

Old gardens are part of the heritage of our islands; they are valuable treasures which so easily become a wilderness if neglected for any length of time.

So we travel between our two homes and their gardens throughout the year. The journey is never dull for the road follows the long high-lying valley where waters of infant Tweed emerge from marshes and springs above Tweedshaw, Neil Manning's roadside farm-steading. From thence we travel over the top of the hillside and the splendour of mile upon mile of rolling Border hills, downhill to Moffat, often picnicking in the car above the Beef Tub, where we can see first glimpses of Blencathra and Skiddaw on clear days. At length we cross the little river Sark into Cumberland and so home to Dalemain to begin another day.

There is always something new and exciting to see at either end of the journey, something worthwhile to do. A little cluster of colour in the garden, which was not there the previous week: some tiny wonder of perfection, which made one's heart leap for joy: that moment of unexpected ecstasy one experiences when a lark soars Heavenward from moorland acres, or when one hears the first cuckoo in spring. A gateway is unexpectedly opened, leading us on to unknown heights. Then one knows contentment, and, that all our efforts for the love of two gardens has been worth while.

RUSTLE OF SPRING

It is the first sweet stirs of spring —
She truly is a lovely thing
Hark! rustling leaves along her way —
Those tiny leaves are turned to press
Their face to feel the sunlight bless
And wake a myriad buds each day.

I hear the rustle of her skirt
Worn woodland worlds become alert
Gnarled, knotted elm tree branches bend
Like courtiers in her royal train,
Fair messengers abroad they send
On fleeting chords of passing rain.

While thrushes lead triumphant song
Shy birds return where they belong,
Sweet willow warblers magic note
Fills river banks with joy unfurled
Where flower filled seeds are borne afloat
As spring lights up the wintry world.

The panoramas golden hours
High fleecy clouds, rich rosy dawn;
Sunlight stretching through the flowers
Pale patterned carpets newly born.
She comes, she warms, she brings new heart,
I'm welled with joy, each minute flies.
Cling to her skirt, ne'er let her part,
For diamonds sparkle in her eyes.

1989

THE LOVE OF POETRY

I've always loved poetry, ever since I was a little girl; so did Mother and her father, Grandpa Stroyan, who lived at Lanrick on the great river Teith beyond Doune, not far from "Glenartney's hazel shades", and whom we saw a great deal. It must have been from these two, particularly Mother, that I acquired my love of rhythm, and the mind pictures it creates.

Living in our beautiful, old-fashioned, slow-moving countryside, funny little nursery rhymes, sometimes their ribald versions, were readily there to Mother such as . . .

> "How doth the little busy bee
> Delight to buzz and bite;
> She gathers honey all the day,
> Then eats it up at night."
> (Last line to be said fast tempo)

Its true version by Isaac Watts (1674-1748) which we also knew just as well, runs,

> "How doth the little busy bee
> Improve each shining hour;
> And gather honey all the day
> From every opening flower."

At a very early age, about five, I went to learn elocution with a charming lady, a former actress. She lived in Arthur Street, one of those hilly streets in Penrith, ascending to the Beacon. There I had the happiest afternoons, once a week, away from Nanny Campbell and nursery routine.

The first thing I learnt was "The King's Breakfast" by A. A. Milne, full of theatrical actions which made everything such fun — "he s-l-i-d down the banisters" . . . bump!

Next came Edward Lear's "The Owl and the Pussy Cat." I can recite these two delicious pieces of nursery literature, and many more, to all our grandchildren, who always ask for more, with the greatest of ease.

Mother encouraged me to recite with action for special visitors, for she enjoyed taking part in amateur theatricals. These recitation antics were not quite so funny for me, unless it was for her brother John, whose whole face became a smile, or for Grandpa; both never failed to give me a tip.

When I was five, Miss Mary Scott came daily to teach James and Anthony Lowther, and myself. She also lived in Arthur Street. On Mondays, Wednesdays and Fridays, Fred Leveratt, our very tall young chauffeur, motored Miss Scott and myself to Clifton Hill, where we had such happy days, interluded with dear Mrs Lowther's surprise outdoor activities. Muriel Lowther, later Viscountess Lowther, had the most wonderful way with young people, and they continually gathered round her to the end of her days. She was a close friend of Mother's from their childhood. Tuesdays and Thursdays, Crisp, the Lowthers' uniformed chauffeur, brought the return party to Dalemain.

With Miss Scott's splendid way of teaching small children, I began to write little verses. Mother was thrilled and one of these was sent to the *Herald* by our dear governess. It was duly published by the editor, Mr Sarginson, who always wrote under the name of Silverpen.

When I was "rising" fourteen, as Father said, likening our years to a young horse, I was sent off to school at Downe House in Berkshire, miles away, but where I really began to learn so much, all so new and wonderful. Miss Olive Willis was the most amazing headmistress of the old school, who collected talented people around her auspicious person to teach music, literature and every form of learning. There was a marvellous library, concert hall, studio and laboratories, besides the chapel. Other people of equal talent were on the staff: Miss Nichol, who had escaped from the Russian Revolution to become the architect and builder of many new school buildings. She always wore long Russian clothes and a tall hat. The Greek theatre was her work, which soon came to life.

A Czech professor and his wife were somehow helped to Britain by Miss Willis and given refuge: he taught us fascinating European cultural history, from a wheelchair, his tortured legs hidden below a rug. Other girls from Germany and Austria were educated with the rest of us. Miss Willis had six white Samoyed dogs to whom she was devoted; so it was she who told me tragic news of my Fell Pony, Tinker. The Greenside bus, driving past Dalemain for the dawn shift in the blackout, the war having just begun, ran into our three Clydesdales and my black pony, breaking the pony's legs: someone had left the wicket gate open. Miss Willis treated the happening like a death in the family and was truly comforting. She already seemed to understand much of the tragedies of war, now beginning to take place in our very own country.

Miss Willis held a doctorate of theology among other things, and prepared us all for confirmation in a profound way, frequently through the world of nature. My father, on his infrequent visits to take me out at weekends, listened enrapt to her sermons on Sundays.

My eyes and ears were opened to so much, and I shall ever be grateful to this wonderful, learned and very human lady.

It was here that I learnt to appreciate some of the poetry of Keats and Shelley, and particularly the indescribable beauty of the words of Gerard Manley Hopkins: his use of words and power of alliteration has remained with me all these years and whose expressiveness I must follow. One very particular piece of his poetry is imprinted on my mind:

THE WINDHOVER

TO CHRIST OUR LORD

I caught this morning morning's minion, king-
    dom of daylight's dauphin, daple-dawn-drawn Falcon,
      in his riding
   Of the rolling level underneath him steady air, and
      striding

High there, how he rung upon the rein of a wimpling wing
In his ecstasy! then off, off forth on swing,
    As a skate's heel sweeps smooth on a bow-bend: the hurl
        and gliding
    Rebuffed the big wind. My heart in hiding
Stirred for a bird, — the achieve of, the mastery of the thing!

Brute beauty and valour and act, oh, air, pride, plume here
    Buckle! *and* the fire that breaks from thee then, a billion
Times told lovelier, more dangerous, O my chevalier!

    No wonder of it: sheer plod makes plough down sillion
Shine, and blue-bleak embers, ah my dear,
    Fall, gall themselves, and gash gold-vermilion.

To me this conveys all the imagery of flower-filled meadows in early summer's dawn: the kestrel away up there — hovering, the beat of his wings keeping him aloft: to me it is pure magic.

One can only write or dream up poetry at certain, unknown moments: sometimes in the small hours. If one has no pen and paper handy, probably kept in the bathroom, the rhythm vanishes: those precious moments of inspiration are seldom possible to recapture, however wonderful they sounded in one's wakening mind.

A CHILD'S THOUGHT OF SPRING

Spring has come this very day
And brought her flowers which are so gay
The sun doth shine with all his might
To make the little flowers look bright.

While primrose, daisy, buttercup
And other flowers come creeping up,
Above them is the sky, so blue,
Makes all below a wondrous hue.

Written when I was seven
Spring 1929

PART I

The turning year,
those chill, uncertain
weeks of waiting.

NEW YEAR RESOLUTIONS IN THE GARDEN

January 1985

As each New Year comes and goes we make so many good resolutions for the months ahead in the garden when the ground is too hard to work. This is the best time to plan alterations for the future. In summertime when borders are overflowing with abundance, one constantly thinks, "I must move this or that plant" to give it, or something else, more room to develop and show itself off to better advantage; and so often nothing is done. One can *always* improve one's garden; group plants together, instead of having them dotted here and there; three or five of a kind look much more effective and give bold splashes of colour while beauty and bone structure of others will cause each group to be more readily appreciated.

Make a plan of your garden on paper, even separate sheets for each border, writing clearly the names of shrubs and plants. Labels are something of a problem unless one is prepared to have them engraved which is expensive, for most labels last only a relatively short while, and especially with rare shrubs and trees, one would like to leave them efficiently labelled for future generations. If paper plans are made and re-drawn when necessary to keep them up to date, a most interesting "diary" of one's garden will be recorded for all time, long after present day labels have broken or disappeared.

"After-care" of plants is equally important. It is useless to plant treasured purchases or expensive Christmas presents and expect them to grow untended. Biting winds are their worst enemy, for recently planted shrubs, trees, roses, and the rest, have not had time to put down firm foundations; they become rocked and blown about, water filling the tunnels created round their root systems, not only freezing but possibly killing their victims into the bargain. It is necessary to go round these newly acquired plants, regularly re-firming them and possibly covering the lower regions with fir branches, bracken or leaves, also to make regular inspections of trees and others which may need new stakes or fresh ties to prevent rubbing. They are like one's children growing out of their shoes which, if not renewed, will pinch and hurt. In the same way, branches develop and swell, and old ties cut deeply into their precious cambium layer behind the bark, thus doing irreparable damage.

Wigwams of stakes or strong garden canes erected round and over choice shrubs to which spruce branches, sacking, or anything available can be tied like a tent, are invaluable. Branches are the best medium, allowing air to circulate, yet keeping winds and icy frosts at bay. Some of my treasures which are most difficult to establish in our cold northern climate, such as Japanese maples, have been protected with wigwams for as many as seven winters. Magnolias have even had semi-permanent structures built around them on to which spruce branches are firmly tied down like an overhanging roof each November until they were truly growing. Each shrub or tree acts as a "nurse" plant to its neighbours; when one plans ahead this important fact should always be borne in mind. Magnolias thus sheltered make wonderful places to grow violets and early flowering primroses beneath overhanging branches. One can go on altering and improving indefinitely.

FULL MOON IN FEBRUARY

The midnight moon is riding high,
Riding far realms of dark, deep blue skies;
Waking my dreams as I gently sleep,
Telling me time that I wake up and rise.

Strange moving shadows weave spells on the lawn,
Moon sits aloof with contemptuous glance;
Pencil-lined beech trees keep rhythmical time,
Netted and fretted, they robe for the dance.

Weird witch-like fir trees stand huddled and close,
Tall, pointed peaked hats they whisper their spells;
Clouds hurry onwards in colours that change
Lone owls call softly, — a quiet night foretells.

Moonbeams and moonlight flash flames on my wall,
Message-like murmurings light on my bed;
What was I dreaming and what have they said?
Moondance disturbing my dreaming gold head.

Whence came that light from fresh, far reaching East?
Song thrush clear calling the break of the day,
Chorus of bird song extol me to wake;
Queen of the night-watch commanded away.

February 1989

11

WONDERS OF WINTER

January 1986

The world outside never fails to surprise and enchant, even on cold midwinter days. After frosty nights when the atmosphere is clear and sharp, sunrise is frequently so exciting that it is worth climbing out of a cosy bed in order to watch dawn's brilliance stealing determinedly across the East Fells, wakening sleeping meadows and valleys below. Colours of these early morning skies are frequently an artist's dream: ruby, pink and gold giving depth to rainbow hues. Bare branches of deciduous trees are silhouetted against eastern skies, while the river across the park wakes out of slumbers in that half world of dawn, like a child overwhelmed with delight because it is morning and time to get up. Sparkling sunlight reflects joy and gladness on still pools of water where wild duck, teal and waterhens are already fishing for their breakfasts in rushy beds; ecstatic sunbeams dance on more turbulent waters as crests of currents become lit up, dazzling like an oil lamp in an old farm stable which beckons to weary travellers from afar.

This was the sort of morning to be remembered as I walked round the garden to see that semi-tender shrubs and climbers were properly protected with spruce branches. Christmas trees, cut up into suitable lengths, make excellent protections, instead of wastefully casting them upon a bonfire; later, when plants are in need of staking, why not use them to prop up low growing herbaceous plants. Japanese maples appreciate shelter, and various climbers such as wisteria and eccromacarpus, the Chilean Vine, are more likely to survive if their lower parts, at least, are covered with spruce branches or other material.

Most trees and shrubs we buy, or are given as presents, arrive in containers and are quite safe standing outside in sheltered places until the ground is suitable for planting. If the containers can be buried they are much less likely to dry out, but the ground being like iron when our new ornamental trees arrived made it impossible to do this and they were stood beneath a plum tree whose spreading branches would help to break sharp frosts. In addition, covering the containers with old leaves and branches to give added protection, hardy plants are much less likely to deteriorate outside. One terrible winter, roses arrived, bare-rooted, at the end of the year, and were heeled into a heap of soil within an open potting shed. It was some time before they were planted and meanwhile they had somewhat deteriorated and never grew well. After that experience, I would rather make a hole with an axe into a clamp of leafmould in order to bury bare rooted plants so that they can obtain succour from the atmosphere.

Despite recent hard frosts, some shrubs are already attempting to push forth a few unwise leaf tips. Even *Magnolia stellata*, well established after ten years of steady growth, was showing tiny leaf portions; the buds of *Syringa vulgans* 'Primrose' appeared to be so alive that one could not but notice their urge to wake. Likewise, old daphne bushes were waiting to burst. Never worry if daphnes half topple on their sides, for they will still continue to bloom; exposed roots can be covered with more soil. Laburnums, being shallow rooted, are very similar in habit; should they half succumb to winds and fall, and should their topmost branches be "in the way", they respond well to being pruned back and in due course will send forth young growths from lower down their stems. One old laburnum, half toppled against a grassy bank in the Wild Garden, never fails to be even more beautiful in blossom time in this unlikely pose; two posts can be driven into the ground with a strong crossbar to support unsteady laburnums so long as sacking or tubing is wrapped round the bar to prevent rubbing.

A constant joy at this season are pure white Christmas Roses blooming happily on the north side of a holly hedge. Sheltered from prevailing winds and from summer sunshine, these hellebores thrive in such a position, with leafmould to feed and protect their precious winter flowers. Perhaps holly has some particular additive, for my father-in-law grew a massive bed of these hellebores behind a high holly hedge in his Edinburgh garden which were a never-to-be-forgotten idea. Their black roots give rise to their being called *Helleborus niger*.

Other hellebores are pushing up buds and fresh growth in sheltered places, particularly that rare creamy-green variety, Kochii which is well worth seeking to plant. The Stinking Hellebore, *foetidus*, is already full of apple green flowers and bracts, sheltered again beneath a half standard Victoria plum; its cartwheel leaves, with deeply cut spokes become fantastically beautiful like waterwheels when viewed at a low height against evening skies; they give a winter display for weeks on end, even in sunless corners. Green *H. corsicus* are best seen when tumbling on a low bank; their shining pointed divided leaves appear to be polished like jewels in winter sunlight, toothed and netted with patterns of veins, as if these veins were like the finest needlework; it will not be long before masses of rounded green flowers are a highlight of the garden, their golden stamens giving an added luminous appearance.

Sometimes Lenten Hellebores with purple bells on six inch stems are incorrectly called the Pink Christmas Rose. Frequently attempting to flower about this time of year, there are many different shades of these hellebores; some are lovely pink flushed forms and are well worth searching for when on a busman's holiday looking for something new and not too difficult to grow for one's garden.

There *must* be a change in the weather coming shortly for blackbirds were busily digging for worms among coatings of snow-kissed leaves beneath our gooseberry bushes. Small brown wrens were searching for grubs on apple boughs and jasmine, already golden with glory, was losing that frigid look which plants assume in self defence when frost holds plant-life in its fierce grip. It is an idea to grow jasmine through a hedge of cotoneasters or yew where its long trails give colour early in the year and bring interest to the sombre hedge. I noted this with interest in a small garden on the outskirts of Edinburgh, and thought how sensible it was to make such good use of limited space. After flowering, as with many other shrubs, jasmine should be pruned back to give it time to produce plenty of young shoots which will mature and carry flower buds for next year's blossom. Persistent jasmine plants were flowering on topmost growths in a relatively sunless courtyard outside our kitchen window at New Year, bursting into bloom wherever the sun could warm their buds, bringing joy to all who saw them; eventually lower growths will burst into blossom too.

Chinese witch hazels make unusual displays at this time of year; they prefer to grow in acid ground and perhaps look their most beautiful in open woodlands where holly trees are still a mass of scarlet berries. Witch hazels are not seen very often, but their quaint spidery flowers adorning bare branches make one stand and stare in delight. *Hamemelis mollis*, of Chinese origin, is most usually grown; its pale yellow flowers are backed by claret-coloured calyces, but there are also new varieties from which to choose. Planted with plenty of peat or leafmould their spider-like flowers show up brightly against a covering of snow.

The year has turned; the shortest day is past; the world outside becomes truly exciting with every passing day, as if one is opening a fresh page of a book one is longing to read. The wonder of the winter garden, and especially winter flowering plants, is so awe-inspiring, so beautiful, something that one must never forget or allow to vanish from one's vision; for memory certainly holds the key to the door of spring.

SHADE LOVING BEAUTIES

January 1988

Garden doors are opening to another spring, full of opportunities and the excitement of planting something different, something we hope will not take endless trouble to grow to perfection in our northern climate.

Shrubs and flowering trees are so well worth planting when endless varieties of bulbs and little treasures can be planted within their protection.

Should your garden get little sun, why not grow *Hydrangea petiolaris* to cover unattractive wall space? Its aerial roots will cling to stonework, or else, a piece of clematis netting will give it a helpful start. Flat heads of white flowers smother these plants during summer months. Variegated ivy will bring colour to sunless walls; *Hedera helix* Goldheart is an elegant, small-leaved variety with brilliant centres within rich green foliage. Morello cherries are one of the most useful shrubs for northern aspects; their young slender branches can be trained, fanlike, to cover a wide area where they take up little space, producing clouds of white star-like blossom in late spring, followed by delectable bright red fruit, which, if netted against greedy birds, can be made into delicious jam. Their many stones may be caught in a wide meshed sieve to produce more of a puréed jam which will be safer, and more enjoyable to eat.

Honeysuckles never fail to give pleasure and varieties which will flower in early spring are much appreciated; *Lonicera fragrantissima* has sweetly scented, creamy white bell-shaped flowers, followed by red berries in May.

Flowering quinces, members of the vast rose family, and now named chaenomeles, thrive on north and east aspects, while on sunnier walls will even bloom at Christmas, sometimes bearing edible golden-yellow quinces in autumn. *C* x *superba* 'Knaphill Scarlet' and *C*. x *s*. 'Rowallane' are reliable old varieties; the latter will spread attractively over a wall or bank. Prune back long shoots in September/October to encourage ample flowering. The pure white *C. speciosa* 'Nivalis' will show off large open-faced flowers when tied and spread against squared polythene netting.

One can never forget the delights of winter jasmine, its starlike yellow flowers brightening our winter. Remember to prune after flowering, shortening strongest shoots which have flowered, whilst cutting others close to the old wood. Young shoots are most effective when allowed to "weep" and grow downwards. Others will "run" and root, and these easily form good plants to move to different situations.

Garrya elliptica is a bushy evergreen whose dark shining leaves highlight tassels of greeny-grey silky catkins in midwinter. It thrives on north and east aspects in warm districts but I would rather plant it in a more favourable situation and enjoy the glory of its catkins. Buy male plants; female plants produce shorter catkins, also bearing deep brown purple fruits in long clusters, which are interesting if space allows. Amongst all these winter flowering climbers plant some of the many varieties of clematis, whose fragile stems delight in "host" plants. Climbing by curling their leaf stalks around whatever support is available, and flowering for many months, they bring colour over a very long period. Once more it is important to prune back the wood made in the previous season to just above a strong pair of buds. Stronger growing *C. montana* varieties, the "Mountain Clematis", can be grown up trees where new growths will hang like festoons of pink or white flowers. They will cover walls, and are most useful when growing near a "sun parlour" where, if clematis netting is spread across the glass roof, these *montanas* are strong enough partially to cover the roof, thus keeping off summer's brilliance while you can enjoy reading or taking a meal without wearing dark glasses! Clematis rejoice in cool root runs, so those difficult sunless corners are ideal for them to start life amongst shade loving herbaceous plants, and soon emerge above them in all their glory.

A TIME FOR ALL THINGS

January 1990

"O, wind, if winter comes, can spring be far behind?"

Already evenings are drawing out. After January 8th we reckon two minutes each day is added to precious hours of daylight. Already aconites are resplendent harbingers of spring, while snowdrops point their white spear-like buds towards turbulent skies.

Nevertheless, mid-winter has its moments of special beauty: gazing at old sycamore and beech trees silhouetted against fleeting sunlit skies, appearing to be already covered with swelling green buds ready to burst into unwary leaves in such open weather.

Perhaps it was an illusion of fantasy — a dream. This is the time of year when gardeners and foresters delight in tree surgery, but already sap is rising and one should be wary of cutting thickish stems of such trees as birches and acers which can easily "bleed." Walnuts, magnolias and others can be damaged irreparably now that the year has turned. The prunus family are best pruned much later when first in new leaf; although likely to ooze sap in so doing, this idea is as a precaution against risk of infection by spores of silver-leaf disease. My old friend, Arthur Hellyer, that great horticulturist, wrote to advise me about an old Victoria plum which began to ooze a nasty sticky gum from the lowest part of its trunk in late summer. I was worried about silver leaf, for which the only cure is to burn offending branches; probably the whole tree will die in the end. The white substance in question turned out to be a form of mould, and a good washing with a solution of Jeyes Fluid cured the ailment. In addition invasive herbaceous plants were dug out which prevented air and light circulating. This is a very important action to take where fruit trees, like our own, grow within flower borders. Such plant as *Euphorbia griffithii* 'Fireglow', Chinese lanterns and 'Eau de Cologne' mint are inveterate spreaders and must be kept in check.

Pruning experts now advocate leaving a small "collar" when severing shoots from their point of union with the branch or trunk. Sometimes there is a visible "collar" or slightly raised ring-mark just out from the main stem; otherwise, it is now advocated to imagine a "collar" when cutting; this has proved to be a more satisfactory point of severance.

In an old garden where fruit trees grow as features among shrubs and flowers, one can over-prune, causing trees to lose their potential as things of beauty. If an old tree is beautiful, yet bears little worthwhile fruit, I would rather buy an extra four pounds of plums or whatever, than spoil the artistry of the garden. Remember too, the value of old trees as homes and feeding grounds for countless birds who come and go, warming the cockles of our souls with their song and joy of living.

This is the time of year to be sowing tomatoes, and then sweet peas. Boltons of Birdbrook, Essex, who originally hailed from Warton in Lancashire and from Penrith on Mr Bolton's grandmother's side, always grow a few good tomatoes: we are trying a fairly new F.1 hybrid, 'Virosa'. It is a good cropper with sweet, medium sized fruit and suitable for transplanting into a cold greenhouse.

We have always grown Mr Bolton's sweet peas, and this year intend to grow them in tubes to avoid disturbance, 2 or 3 seeds to a tube. Although it is said to be unnecessary to remove the tubes on planting, we will make a cut right down the container to allow roots to expand easily. Usually our sweet peas are grown in wooden boxes with moss at the bottom of the mixture. They grow extremely well into this medium, but however carefully the young plants are transplanted, the roots are entwined in the moss; necessary disentanglement somewhat slows up their growth. It would be beneficial to put a little sphagnum or other moss at the bottom of each tube, since nothing would be disturbed when planting out.

One winter's morning the most exciting letter arrived from Mr Bolton with whom I had had some correspondence attempting to establish how long, probably before the turn of the century, Stuart had grown this firm's sweet peas. Now, his grandson, Mr Robert Bolton, had two new varieties to be newly listed, and wondered if we would allow them to be called 'Sylvia Mary' and 'Dalemain'.

I could hardly believe my eyes: it was all so exciting, quite unbelievable. I rushed upstairs to Bryce's library to show him the letter and wept with joy on his shoulder. So these two varieties are presently in their 1991 catalogue, and I was told by a sweet pea grower who shows blooms regularly that 'Sylvia Mary' is considered to be the better of the two by his show-minded friends, which to me is just wonderful. This variety, which features on the cover of the catalogue, is a rich shade of rose cerise, with great intensity of colour reflected in the wings, its robust flowers produced in great profusion. 'Dalemain', equally fragrant, is a rich ruby, the flowers of amazing size, produced in abundance; there is even a drawing of Dalemain itself in the catalogue.

In the old days, seedsmen travelled round their gardening friends to collect orders, and I'm sure that Will Stuart produced a bottle of whisky from his potting shed drawer whenever Mr Bolton's grandfather came on his rounds which they drank with compliments of the season in the convivial warmth of his hothouse, or even more likely by the fireside of his house beside the carriage archway, leading out of the courtyard and on to the rough road to Penrith.

Now, a year later, the two varieties look well in tubes, waiting for spring and good weather when they will be planted out. Sweet peas are hardier than people often think; so long as short pea stakes are pushed into the ground to protect them from late frosts, they will grow far better in the ground than left in a cold frame.

When summer comes, and bowls of these two lovely varieties make a picture of fragrant beauty in the drawing room, and perhaps the rich ruby colour of 'Dalemain' glowing within the dark panelling of the Fretwork Room, the Elizabethan parlour in the medieval part of the house, then Mr Bolton's trust in our ability to grow his new varieties will be repaid.

There is still time to order a few exciting new plants. Penstemons have always been a favourite and we are trying the white *P. smallii* 'Snowstorm' said to be a flurry of white trumpets on bushy plants, 75 cm high. These will partially fill a box-wood edged bed in the Knot Garden, together with that lovely, silver-filigreed artemisia, *A. Schmidtiana* 'Nana' and various small pinks. Meanwhile this bed is fringed with a planting of enchantingly lovely Barnhaven double primroses, all grown from seed.

A low growing, golden-leaved shrub took my fancy, *Choisya ternata* 'Sundance' but it needs protection from cold winds and late frosts, so may have to be grown in a large pot in which it will decorate some corner of the garden in due course.

So many of the plants one buys from nursery gardens are not properly hardened off, and would be much safer in a frame or cold greenhouse or set in the ground below a sheltering shrub until the last frosts are over, and only then planted into their allotted places. One is thereby less likely to lose expensive new purchases.

LOVE OF THE LAND

Although these acres far and wide
Are written in my name,
Such gracious fells and fields beside
Were long before I came
To live, and love, and gently care;
Watch o'er this country, sweet and fair.

Fresh waters deep, and sparkling stream,
Brown trout, pied perch and eel,
'Tis where I like to sit and dream
And peaceful moments steal,
Hark to red deer in rutting days,
Watch nature's all mysterious ways.

But when I hear the brown owls call
Safe perched in golden trees,
Feel autumn's winds rise, play and fall
Leaves dance around my knees;
Before wild storms of winter blow
When all I love is dressed in snow.

These lovely woods we've set in store
We've planted, weeded, sown,
As generations gone before
Have done the best they've known.
We've laid hay harvest lands to rest,
For fields and flocks we've done our best.

Each treasure of this countryside
Left in our temp'ral care;
Gnarled shelt'ring trees shield pastures wide,
Green valleys, quiet and fair.
Buttercups golden and deep, drilled corn,
Sweet marshy meadows where flowers are born.

Soon, all too soon, each year slips past,
Till these lands will belong to our son
Who will do his best to the very last
In the way all our forbears have done.
Our days will be past, though time has flown,
Will we still care, in "The Great Unknown?"

Bluebells in Stainton Wood

Aconites at Dalemain in February

Knot Garden and Roman Fountain at Dalemain

A HAVEN OF HEDGES

February 1987

Protection from winds and draughts is the greatest necessity for plant life; whether your garden be large or small, winds means devastation to so many growing things. Hard frost does untold good, however much we dislike the cold as human beings, but Jack Frost breaks up the soil, leaving it in a better state when spring comes, urging plant life into energetic growth. Frost is particularly beneficial if a previous fall of snow wraps one's treasures with an insulating blanket. Will Stuart taught me so much which has stood in good stead for all my many gardening years. He was head gardener at Dalemain until his death in 1946, having started as a young, fully trained enthusiast fifty years previously, when Uncle John and his Irish wife, Aunt Maud, lived at Dalemain in considerable style. When digging my first trench as a child, Stuart urged me to open out my trench and leave it thus for some weeks to allow weather to break up hidden depths; it was after these weeks that rotted farm manure was put into the trench, leaf mould or even old cabbage leaves, and then filled in. A good dressing of bone meal was scattered on the surface which takes six months to really work as a tonic: as a result of all these labours, what wonderful blooms we produced.

Will Stuart, head gardener at Dalemain, caught by
Sylvia Hasell's Box Brownie, c. 1930.

In the north, we are wise enough to grow hardy trees and plants unless we are prepared to give other unreliable delights adequate shelter. Being prudent and provident Northerners, we usually invest in plants that will survive severe winters; even these will grow ten times better if sheltered from the blast.

Have you ever thought of planting hedges within your garden? Not the exquisite hedges of hawthorn, blackthorn or hazel and the like that still divide some of our fields, growing upon well-made, cast-up banks of earth and stone, but hedges of shrub and species roses, cotoneaster, berberis, boxwood and so many more. Hedges do not necessarily require unlimited room, and can be trimmed annually to keep them within required limits.

One of the loveliest hedges I know is composed of the ancient Chinese species rose, *R. farreri*, discovered by Reginald Farrer on one of his famous plant hunting expeditions to the Far East.

The tiny pink flowers, giving rise to its picturesque name, the Threepenny Bit Rose, cover the hedge for many weeks, while minute thorns make it eminently suitable for keeping unwanted animals at bay. Long ago I bought one plant: having always been fascinated by propagating and increasing stock, cuttings were taken in early autumn and dibbled into holes filled with sharp sand to encourage them to survive and root. One cannot expect every cutting to grow, but if more than sufficient are "taken", it is not disastrous if only fifty per cent grow to maturity. This hedge, and other "occasional" plants are lovely all seasons, whether winter's hoar frost sparkles like diamonds on numerous minute branches, or sunshine lights up the tiny saucer like flowers.

Boxwood hedging has been practised for hundreds of years. Elizabethan gardeners created their knot gardens with small beds of varying shapes, each edged with the smaller leaved, yellow-green *Buxus sempervirens* 'Suffruticosa' variety which is the true 'edging box'; these knot gardens were sometimes created to reflect the pattern of plaster ceilings in their house. Here within these beds they grew herbs of many kinds which were desperately needed, not only for culinary purposes, but also for medical reasons. It is quite surprising, when reading about the history of plants, to discover how many were used in these ways, while with modern medicines one scarcely realises their early and true values.

Berberis is a valuable family, easy of cultivation and versatile in both colour and manner of growth. *B. thunbergii atiopurpurea* 'Roseglow' is a very striking form, its young growth suffused with silver-pink and rose colours turning to purple. Being slow growing I have used it as a dwarf hedge to shelter rock plants and also as an individual shrub planted at each corner of our water-lily pool with effective charm. *Berberis x stenophylla*, 'Cream Showers', makes a more vigorous plant with upright arching branches festooned with creamy white, bell-shaped flowers. All these plants used for hedging should be trimmed lightly each year, following flowering, but only after they have become well established. Trimming keeps hedges neat and avoids unnecessary bare patches.

Soil should be well prepared before planting and if possible farmyard manure or leafmould dug into clean ground. If established hedges are fed from time to time they will bring colour, glory and shelter to your garden.

Many other ornamental shrubs can be planted, pyracantha being used frequently on the continent. These Firethorns, both *P*. 'Orange Glow' and *P*. 'Soleil d'Or', blossom effectively followed by wonderful displays of berries which are frequently a feast for birds, but I never grudge these inhabitants of our gardens a good feed; they do untold good by catching insects and pollinating flowers, besides waking us up at first light to tell us that spring is just around the corner. One can put a light net over highly regarded berries, so long as the birds are provided with plenty of other foods.

A last thought is to create a hedge of lavender, the old scented *Lavandula angustifolia* 'Munstead' variety, particularly if you require something low and bushy. Plant this in a sunny, reasonably well-drained position, and after the first two years of growth trim fairly hard in early April to produce both neatness and an abundance of flowers. The delicious old-world scent will make your friends want to emulate your handiwork. Do remember to "take" a few cuttings early in the autumn to provide against hard winter and its consequent losses.

ON VALENTINE'S DAY

Dear aconites, your precious flowers
Rejoice these days of frosted hours.
When you arise you wake sweet spring
And make our two hearts glad to sing.

While snowdrops, fair as pearly dawn
Renew our love with light reborn:
Their dream bells ring, each play their part,
I'll always hold you in my heart.

February 14th 1990

CANDLEMAS BELLS

It does not matter, sweet snowdrops
Though you are most dreadfully late,
For you raise my heart in the morning
When sunshine smiles in through the gate.

That gate 'mong the dark green pine trees,
Where sunbeams a-dazzle with light,
Shine on your petals, sweet snowdrops
Cause winter to sing with delight.

Though snow lies as soon as a carpet
Deep piled in the depths of the wood,
Spring urged you to grow in the darkness
Amongst russet leaves where you stood.

Winters last long on our hillsides,
But precious bells, guarded and true,
Ready to rise in the dawning
Your fairy caps spangled with dew.

Chiming your bells in the springlight,
Urging shy, late buds to swell
Praising the break of the dawning
Ringing your Candlemas bell.

March 1989

GLORIES OF THE WINTER GARDEN

February 1989

In winter months gardens need never be considered dull or unattractive, for they have an alluring quality equal to summer's bounty: the countryside seems even more endearing when sunlight reflects through leafless trees, or dances upon water, whether it be a chattering stream beside a nearby garden or a river flowing steadily, and rhythmically. One appreciates the little things that stand out with intrinsic beauty when they are not cluttered.

One of the most beautiful things I saw of late was an elderly Chinese witch hazel growing in a cousin's garden beside harmonious waters of the River Teith. This *Hamamelis mollis* was simply covered with clusters of golden-yellow flowers whose sweetly fragrant, spidery petals scented the whole garden.

The original Chinese witch hazel, a choice, more spreading form, *H.M.* 'Coombe Wood', was introduced by C. Maries in 1879: it has yellow autumn colouring, and a strong, sweet fragrance. Witch hazels are very hardy, but I try to site them in sheltered warm situations, where they can be enjoyed to the full. There are many forms, one of the choicest being H. japonica 'Sulphurea' with crumpled pale sulphur yellow flowers: *H.* x *intermedia* 'Jelena', also known as 'Copper Beauty' or 'Orange Beauty', has autumn colours of orange, red and scarlet. A beautiful newer selection of fragrant *H. mollis* is 'Pallida' with really fragrant flowers, invaluable in winter weeks. Numerous, sizeable flowers of clear, bright yellow are followed by golden yellow leaves in autumn. It can grow to be 150-200 cm if planted in the right position, but never forget, they dislike limy conditions.

Our native species is truly impressive also when draped with long yellow catkins; these are the lambs' tails for which we always look in February. This species belongs to the corylus family, many being cultivated for their edible nuts, particularly valuable in long ago days. The 'filbert', grown for its large nuts, was imported from the Balkans in 1759.

A cotoneaster well worth planting is *C.* x *Watereri* 'Exburiensis' in half-standard form; very similar to *C.* x *W.* 'Rothschildianus', its wide spreading branches bear large clusters of apricot-yellow fruits which appear almost cream at this time of year. Bees are readily attracted to their flowers and it seems that birds leave the berries alone, while they rob most other forms of their red berries. The white clusters are extremely eye-catching, especially when standing taller than other plants and shrubs.

There is a cotoneaster to suit almost any situation; low spreading forms make ideal cover for bulbs to push their way and be protected from icy blasts or from birds, particularly pheasants, who relish tulip bulbs. Charming blue *Anemone obtusiloba* are thankful for a little protection of such shrubs. Forming neat little clumps of small buttercup-like flowers with radiating stems, they flower over a long period from early spring, depending on the weather, and are at their best growing in cool acid soils. Mine have been in flower for a long time and are always a joy to behold. There are also rarer white and pink forms.

Other forms of anemones with neat rhizomes or corms spread easily when contented with their situation. They are mostly relations of the wind flower. One of the choicest is a yellow form given to me many years ago by an aunt who was a great gardener. She created a wonderful garden on what had been an open hillside near Broughton: there was always friendly rivalry as to whether her garden or our own at Huntfield was the higher above sea level! Some of these rare yellow anemones have also spread their golden glory at Dalemain, appearing happily around roots of rose bushes and the like. The blue species *A. blanda* is a very early flowerer and is excellent among rock plants.

Whenever I have bulbs to spare which enjoy woodland conditions, some are moved to "wild gardens" where they can spread at random amongst leaves and rotted bark.

Aconites are the most wonderful colonizers and once established colonies of hardy two-leaved seedlings appear in truly wintery weeks whose seeds will form corms to flower two years hence.

Before January had said farewell, there were little rock irises in full flower, an occasional daffodil and masses of crocuses brightening our borders.

If you should buy herbaceous plants such as delphiniums, it would be advisable to keep them in a cold frame until mid March. So many plants, sold as hardy, have been forced by their growers for the market and winter weeks may still bring cold and chill.

Candlemas Day began with sunshine, lighting up the most unexpected corners, particularly where greening clematis were rambling up rough pink sandstone walls of the oldest part of Dalemain. As the day wore on, skies became darkened with stormy clouds and winds, a reminder that winter can easily damage precocious plants.

THE DEVIL'S BEEF TUB

The Devil is stirring his kalepot
And the witches are dancing with glee;
Curls of mist writhe out of his beef tub
As he stokes for his evening tea.

For evening winds are chilly
As we labour the steep hill pass;
October is borne with a flourish
Where frost lies alive on the grass.

We are lost in the smoke of his caldron;
The hillside grows steeper, until
We are out on the fair green summit
Of this timeless, eternal hill.

Far below, from the depths of his beef tub
A mocking mysterious call
As he stokes with an old fashioned pallet
While mists rise with rhythm, and fall.

Black-faced gimmers march upwards
Away from the de'il and his wrath;
Together we drive home e're darkness,
Treading this well-worn path.

DREAMING OF ACONITES

March 1985

Spring is hurrying into every corner of our countryside faster than we can almost realise. Since the weeks prior to Christmas aconites have been peeping up towards wintery skies in many corners of our gardens where shelter is the prime factor for early flowering subjects. These harbingers of spring love cosy open woodland conditions where the sun can shine, and fringes of trees or shrubs keep fierce winds at bay; for weeks the little Grove close to the house has been a sheet of gold, as if angels have spread the glory of their mantles to cheer all who pass by with the promise of a wakening earth.

Always my favourite flowers since I can first remember, they have an extraordinary pattern of behaviour; a first sheet of buds and flowers emerge, and as these pass for another season, a second kirtle takes place; they flower for weeks, until the beginning of April, when, quite suddenly, they are past. Meanwhile, as petals fall five small seed capsules form a tiny coronet within their curved tips reaching upwards, pointing Heavenwards to the sunbeams which are already swelling their capsules of minute seeds with fruition.

In a very few weeks the ground surrounding each cluster of spent blooms will be covered with two-leaved seedlings which will grow into nutty brown corms to flower two years hence. Besides these, small frilly one-year-olds cover corners like ballet dancers wearing fresh green skirts above slim pinky-green stems. The Grove, these few weeks later, has been filled with snowdrops which woke more sleepily than their yellow neighbours. In places periwinkles grow, their long green trails helping to conserve moisture in the hottest summer.

Eventually, no one would suspect what wealth of gold lies hidden beneath summer's jungle of wild loveliness — cow-parsley, wild arums, ragged robin and speedwells.

These little corms are better lifted in their own earth, as bought ones seem to lose much of their viability when removed from natural habitats. This fact came forcibly in our first tiny garden in Ayrshire. *Of course* we must have winter's wondrous blessing in our very own garden; so often one tries to emulate all manner of things one loved as a child. Aconite corms were duly bought from Austin MacAslan's seed merchant's shop in Glasgow, few of which came to life, even though they were planted most carefully. The following year little clusters were dug from the Grove before they all disappeared too deeply for another year. Transported in shoe boxes they rooted readily in our garden.

One never ceases to learn; from every garden one passes on the roadside there is nearly always something beautiful one would like to copy. Now, as I write from a hospital bed, there is time to dream about our two gardens, with two tumblers of aconites at my bedside carefully picked by the family to promote a speedy recovery.

What strikes forcibly when illness comes unexpectedly, as it comes to most people at some time in life, is that sick gardeners realise sadly the vulnerability of small precious treasures. As one becomes less able, one must use ground cover and permanent plants, easy caring climbers which, in clothing walls will provide shelter and security for more fragile clematis or members of the rich coloured vine family. From years of devoted gardening I soon learned that every plant must have a "nurse plant" to help it to give of its best. When I return home, the tumblers of aconites, already forming seed, are going with me; perhaps they are not fully ripe, but they will be scattered beneath a huge Azalea Mollis near the house so that they will have every chance of resurrection in another spring.

CARPETS OF EARLY BULBS
AND A VERY SPECIAL FUND

April 1988

Living between two gardens, one hundred miles apart, has some unexpected and rewarding advantages, perhaps the chief being that one has veritably two springs, following each other a fortnight apart.

Huntfield, on the north side of rolling Scottish uplands, is burdened with long cold winters, causing the delights of spring to arrive much later than on somewhat lower ground at Dalemain. There, first aconites show golden faces from among thickets of lilac on the edge of sheltering woodlands by New Year's Day, followed by snowdrops. These are truly Candlemas bells ringing in the feast of Candlemas and ever earlier daylight; a most important season to celebrate from earliest times.

The winter of 1987-88, being so unlike our usual snowy and icy season, caused aconites and snowdrops to lose their glory by mid-March, returning to seed-producing greenery. How sad, I thought, for these winter flowers are very precious; but when we returned to Huntfield they were still in full glory, even celebrating Easter in conjunction with first daffodils and sky-blue scillas.

Each morning when taking my two small dachshunds for a run, we go into nearby open woodlands where bulbs of many varieties can multiply at will. It is worth every minute to wander among carpets of double snowdrops; very few are singles in our Scottish garden, though quite the opposite across the border.

There are many species of snowdrops besides the two we know so well. While reading *A Flower for Every Day* by that knowledgeable lady gardener, Margery Fish, I was astounded to read her descriptions of double snowdrops which she describes as frequently coarse "except for those two gems, G. 'Poe' and G. 'Miss Hassell'." Could this last named be a rare snowdrop discovered by my great grannie, or the great aunts who delighted in making woodland gardens by the water's edge? Names were frequently spelt in different ways in the old days, and this Miss Hassell, who I later discovered lived in Cambridge, might have been some distant connection.

Nothing daunted, I searched for a "different" snowdrop in a once much-loved woodland garden whose focal point was the King Oak — an enormous tree with a seat around its trunk. Here I played as a child and remembered carpets of snowdrops near-by. Eventually after much searching, I noticed a few clusters of doubles and some of these were very different with three inner petals shaped like tiny rowing boats hanging below the out-skirt of petals. Perhaps these flowers really were Miss Hassell's gem! Not long after I learned that Margery Fish's friend only died about 1950, while my discovery was certainly of a much earlier date, and doubly special. This year our Dalemain snowdrops lived up to their calling and occasional clusters also appeared in the walled garden in two places. A few blooms were packed carefully and posted by special delivery to Chris Bricknell, recognized snowdrop expert and Director General of the Royal Horticultural Society. He was most interested and replied saying that there was no reason why "our" snowdrop should not be called the Dalemain Snowdrop to distinguish it, and this will of course link it to the garden. This really was a most exciting find.

Early bulbs are seeding magnanimously, so do give your bulbs a chance to do likewise, being careful not to fork where they grow happily. Scillas have become sky-blue carpets at Huntfield, but an indifferent michaelmas daisy has taken up residence among some of these bulbs and the only way to be rid of the nuisance is to lift clumps complete with scillas, depositing the entire forkful within the perimeter of beech trees, using a spade to make convenient holes. Here, they can seed freely to produce further carpets of blue, amongst well-established pink dog-tooth violets.

Already clusters of the magnificent cream species are pushing up in both gardens, making my heart leap for joy whenever I see them. This species *Erythronium revolutum* 'White Beauty' often bears two flowers with reflexing petals on each stem, set among richly coloured foliage.

Miniature narcissi are exquisite among rock plants at this time of year; most of them flower early. Minimus, with tiny trumpets, soon establishes itself into small clusters of bulbs, which eventually may be replanted as single bulbs when leaves are dying back, but still "in the green." Yellow hooped petticoat, Narcissus 'Angel's Tears', 'N. Dove Wings', and many more small and graceful species, some fragrant, are well worth planting. Left undisturbed like so many other spring bulbs they will multiply to give abundant pleasure in the years ahead.

THE MIRACLE OF SPRING

Springtime is wondrous beautiful
All clean and fresh and always good;
Each tree new robed in fairest green,
Unfurling quietly where they would.

Clear clouds reflecting on the hills
Like angels, whisper as they pass
Across those azure skies of spring
They dance upon pure sweet young grass.

Blackthorn in blossom, strikes a chord,
Charmed cherries lilt to what they say;
Sharp sunlight falls upon the ash
While hedgerows sing their songs of May.

Warmed willow catkins, silver grey
Rejoice with warblers heart-filled song;
While swallows skim dark deep'ning pools
Where buds are gold as days grow long.

Oh, how I love to dream and stare
My heart is lithesome, longs to sing;
Watch tiny miracles unfold
Perfection of a newborn spring.

Spring 1989

TOO MUCH SUN MAKES A DESERT

There are "difficult" corners in almost every garden, but the choice of plants available is so great that invariably there are suitable subjects for even areas one thinks quite hopeless.

There are two particular areas in our garden relatively sunless, which formerly posed as difficult problems, for they are corners which are in constant view and would give an immediate feeling of neglect if they were abandoned. The first is a pocket-handkerchief garden surrounded by two walls, an ancient stable and a dense wood. It was here that my granny made a Victorian rockery with ferns; but in these latter days and in its place, a two-sided border has become a thing of beauty and a joy to all who constantly pass that way. Firstly, the walls. Clematis delight in having their roots in shade and their flowers in the sun, so *C. montana rubens* was an obvious choice, quickly growing through *Cotoneaster simonsii* which had been planted and clipped reasonably close against one wall; the clematis leans over coping stones, pouring their loveliness like a waterfall for all to see. Likewise, Virginia creeper sends up trails of scarlet strands, while the cotoneaster's brilliant berries feed hungry birds during winter months.

Morello cherries like to grow on a north facing wall, and one of these produces flowers and fruit on the stable wall; honeysuckle and a beautiful small leaved ivy called 'Golden Heart', and *Hydrangea pitiolaris*, the climbing variety, are beginning to clothe the other, but in such a situation plants and climbers all need feeding each spring.

Rodgersias are ideal for carpeting cool sunless corners; horse chestnut shaped leaves of *R. pinnata*, *R. palmatum's* handsome leaves colour attractively forming eye-catching weed-smothering groups. Hellebores, Solomon's seal, columbines and, best of all, handsome black spires of *Ligularia przewalskii* stand like church spires above ornamental foliage, each spire clothed with small chrome yellow flowers, making this an outstanding plant for cool borders; they multiply wondrously for such a specially good and little known variety of the ornamental Senecio family. A young home-grown plant of a statuesque spurge was planted not long ago. *Euphorbia wulfenii* forms a glaucous evergreen bush with ornamental sulphur-yellow heads, needed to enliven this corner.

Epimedium pinnatum colchicum is a beautiful, low growing, shade-loving plant whose leaflets are marbled with rosy colourings after pale yellow flowers have completed their visitation.

Well-loved Dusty Millers, *Primula auricula*, make full use of shaded conditions and good drainage along the edge of the gravelled path. Extra leafmould sprinkled in among their brittle stems as leaf-buds develop in late spring encourages them to layer themselves and grow more profusely. When pricking out a packet of seedlings, it is worth remembering that the smallest of their numbers are usually the choicest colours; this is true of many types of plants produced from seed. Protecting this narrow border clipped boxwood hedging forms a sweet scented barrier. Boxwood grows easily from cuttings dibbled into slip trenches in early autumn, cut surfaces being lightly dipped in rooting powder during this inexpensive operation to form hedging much beloved in earlier days. Cuttings take a full year to form rooting systems before they begin to grow, but it is well worth waiting for final results.

A small central courtyard came into being in the middle of our ancient home when further walls and buildings were added to the twelfth century pele tower throughout later centuries. Once more, little sun reaches this garden. Shaded by high roofs and numerous chimney stacks, it is something of a frost hollow in addition. To my surprise phloxes grow magnificently. Siberian wallflower has a long colourful season; blue-eyed Marys, the forget-me-not-like *Brunera macrophylla*; lily of the valley, *Begonia semperflorens* and of course *Ligularia przewalskii* which grow statuesque and magnificent. Once again clematis enjoy these conditions; a young *C. tangutica* from seed, already scrambling up bare stems of a climbing rose, its fluffy silver-green old man's beard seed heads an added glory to this Chinese clematis.

Each winter barrow loads of manure or some fresh soil mixture are wheeled into this small courtyard through the back door and across plastic bags laid on the floor of the medieval hall, to ensure that plant life will be well nurtured to give of its best and bring joy to many people despite the difficulties of growing conditions. Sometimes a challenge brings fresh ideas into our lives.

WINTER'S DAYBREAK

Red robin wakes up early
Just at the break of day
When skies are pink and pearly
He sings his round-a-lay.

His friend within a lilac bush
Gives back an answering call
With haste the two together rush
To sing upon our wall.

From dense, dark firs o'er yonder
Wise old owl gives answering call
"A fox is on the wander
Heed! He'll come and chase you all."

Now other birds begin to sing
Those robins do not care
The morning's like a day in spring
Glad sunbeams warm the air.

Old owl calls, "Well, I'm off to bed"
Small wrens give sweet reply
While blackbird from the potting shed
Watch seagulls drift the sky.

Frail ferns in fairy patterns stay
Where leafless trees strange shadows cast
Bird footprints trace the dazzling lawn
The frosted night a thankful past.

PART II

Early Summer's Magic
When pearly dewdrops mirror the magic
of Early Summer's Wonderland

UNEXPECTED TREASURES

May 1987

The wonderful spell of summer-like weather that warmed our countryside in April brought untold numbers of seedlings to life, many quite unexpectedly. In fields beyond the precincts of the gardens, barley, barely in the ground, germinated in record time, but on May 2nd, as we might have expected, snow fell steadily on high ground. Even as we peered out in the early morning, a snow storm raged and the countryside was white for a few hours.

When the comfortable covering had disappeared, an enormous number of unexpected seedlings were still growing steadily; the most unusual were those of *Veratrum viride*, the stately tall yellow-green hellebore sprouting happily in rough grass and in borders. These False Hellebores, forming large clusters of onion-like bulbs, are truly magnificent, particularly in wild garden conditions where their great, broad-ribbed leaves are crowned with tall spires of pale yellow flowers growing upon small stemlets extending from the whole length of their strongly made eye-catching stems. The name veratrum is ancient, there being a dark leaved *V. nigrum* and also *V. album* with creamy white flowers. Native of Austria and the Caucasus country, they grow in various situations, quickly forming eye-catching clusters of ornamental spires, flowering happily in sun or shade in both our gardens at Dalemain and at Huntfield, preferring moisture retaining surroundings. They are no trouble to grow, but I would advise readers to buy a plant, which should increase rapidly, rather than depend on germinating seeds. Never before have I seen so many strong seedling plants, two to three inches tall; they must revel in these warm April conditions. Cherries, too, have germinated freely of their own free will, and would be used at a later date to plant as wind-breaking hedges which would be a helpful addition to many gardens.

The most exciting germination has been of damp-loving primulas. Each autumn I watch for seed heads of many varieties to ripen, at which time they are sown in wooden tomato boxes and left to the care of wind and weather in a sheltered corner. I use our own riddled soil mixed with leafmould and sharp sand or gravel. Seeds are scattered freely of wondrous varieties such as helodoxa, the yellow Himalayan cowslip which produces bell-shaped flowers in summer; *Primula denticulata*, the drumstick primula, its colours varying from lavender, rosy pink, to white. A light covering of soil mix protects newly sown seeds, while a few stalks and flower heads remain on top to help identify varieties in case labels disappear through winter weeks. When seedlings are large enough to handle, I use an old dinner fork to prick out some of them, while others are planted out in little groups, there being so many, but I am loath to waste anything so lavishly bestowed by nature. If you have a damp patch in your garden there is nothing so rewarding as candelabra primulas and others of this fascinating tribe; if not unduly disturbed, beyond careful weeding, primulas of many varieties will rewardingly emulate their colourful parents. The sensational *P.* 'Inverewe', which easily forms goodly clumps in congenial soil, is a hybrid not setting true seed; its numbers can be increased by division, the plantlets easily parted when they are on the move in spring. Tubular, bright orange-red flowers are held proudly, on stems coated with white farina. One of the loveliest of the Chinese primulas, *P.sieboldii*, produces lilac and white flowers covered with farina; their pale green, jagged leaves give equal pleasure as they emerge from the underworld in April; it was discovered by Siebold the traveller and botanist. It is well worth transporting sacks of acid soil and leafmould to cover suitable patches, if one's garden is composed of alkaline soil. Good colour forms can be easily reproduced by careful division in late spring. The pleasure one absorbs from such successful toils is worth every effort. Do look out for worthwhile seedlings in your gardens, and cosset these "treasures from Heaven."

EARLY MORNING IN MAY

Blue skies;
Sunlit skies;
Swallows are wheeling the clear morning sky:
Leaf loving trees,
Flutter the breeze:
Swallows are rising and riding on high.

Old Sandstone ridging tipped warm with rose pink,
Mossed, lichened slate roofs fast shadow and sink.

There in the bathtub I wander and lie
Watch swallows who wheel in a May morning sky.

November 1989

BIRDS IN SPRING

I'd love to be a warbler
And sing in willow trees
Ethereal and wondrous songs
Outspeak the chill March breeze.

An apple tree in blossom
Tied hard against the wall
I'd be a tiny chatt'ring wren
For there I'd pipe and call.

Or if I was a goldfinch
My haunt an old Greek fir
That gives fresh food for all her young
E're other trees confer.

Redshanks stalk flow'ring rushes,
Kingfishermen spy rocks;
Red robins hunt those old gnarled elms
Goldfinch from thistle clocks.

Ducks chatter in the river
While pee-wits wing the plough
But skylarks reach the Heavens
To pledge their unseen vow.

And here they'll sing at daybreak
Then chatter words at dawn
While mistle thrushes speckled breasts
Reflect the lights of dawn.

They'll sing in sweet communion
With birds of every breed;
Blackbirds that perch the stable roof
Sedge warblers from the reed.

Wide shining pools, victorious
With trout and newborn flies
While curlews cry the meadow
Sweet swallows reel the skies.

BLACKTHORN WINTER

May 1988

"Aren't gardeners such nice people?" I was almost hugged by a complete stranger the other afternoon, when Jean Maddison stopped to talk awhile. I was busy amongst precious double primroses. She had wandered round in search of the rarely offered plant *Smilacina racemosa*, of which a young cluster grows in a cool, moist part of the border; its dropping Solomon's-seal-like foliage will soon be eye-catching when crowned with gorgeously fluffy white flowers.

Jean was admiring so many treasures in our garden and I was explaining that it was Aunt Martha Elliott who grew those charming double yellow anemones with twin heads, probably *Anemone ranunculoides* 'Flore Pleno', and had given me a small cluster of their rhizomes many years ago. This energetic lady had created a fascinating garden on a hillside at Broughton Place in Peeblesshire. Aunt Martha and I were always good friends, and she gave me some of my treasured plants which all grow well in both gardens. The yellow anemone, semi-double and very unusual, multiplies their small nobbly brown rhizomes happily in both our gardens: when some of these are roughly pushed out by parent rhizomes they can be moved to start other colonies. So many spring flowering corms increase in this manner.

I talked with my new-found friend about slim-leaved day-lilies which create a continuous display of pale yellow flowers, while their usual broader-leaved brethren seem to be more choosy about the season, although their yellow-green leaves never fail to be ornamental for most of the year. Those of the smaller variety were given to me by our children's nanny, who was with us for many years. She brought them to our Ayrshire home from an elderly friend's garden in Glasgow. Another treasure, a marvellous deep pink shrub rose is still known as Dr Bullock who was minister of Stobo Kirk, and a collector of old roses of local habitation. The most beautiful gentian-blue pulmonaria came from Phyllis Reid-Walker's connoisseur's garden at Biggarshiels. This desirable lungwort, *P.* 'Azure Beauty', carpets the ground from early spring, and in addition becomes a splendid suppressor of weeds with plentiful supplies of leafy foliage to follow.

Jean Maddison was fascinated, for she too is a plantswoman; she reciprocated, telling me of treasures in her own garden near Hexham which are also known by the donor's names. She has a small nursery at Chester-le-Street and finds great pleasure in searching for unusual plants for which customers ask, but she enthralled me talking of her father, grandfather and great-grandfather, all Campbells, who, each in turn, had been head gardeners at Pollok House near Glasgow for the Stirling-Maxwell family. Their seed lists and plant lists for that important garden, dating back to 1820, are still in her safe-keeping. The famous Burrell collection is housed, and on view to the world, in the grounds of Pollok House.

This time of year is the most unpredictable season in the garden, especially after such an open winter. Weeks of mild, frequently wet weather, caused sap to rise much too soon, and buds to swell and burst. It is madness to set out colourful bedding plants, even if one hardens them off; they are not created to stand up to northern frosts, most of them originating from warmer climates. Our native black-thorn is alert to all the vagaries of early spring; its blossom is a wonderful sight at present in many hedgerows or grows free-standing in rough spinnies. Gnarled old trees with shining black branches crowned with pure white flowers are breathtaking-ly beautiful; but never forget that this sight will surely bring the Blackthorn winter of frost and cold. As a child I remember Father and wise people of the countryside speak of "the Blackthorn Winter"; one must never forget that this may occur at such an unpredictable season. Blue berries from this thorn are used for making sloe gin, so it has many uses, not the least being as a hedgerow plant where its sharp thorns keep sheep from wandering. "Whips" from older shrubs can be used to fill in gaps.

Early one open February when I was working on the Terrace, Reg Redhead, who helps on the estate and is a man of many trades, came to ask "What's that white flower growing in the Bay Paddock beside the river?" We could see easily across the park to the river, and there was the startlingly beautiful blackthorn in full flower at a much earlier season than usual. I walked across the park to see these rough old bushes that I knew when I was a child. What a hardy jewel to brighten winter's weariness.

Greenhouses became packed out with seedlings and boxfuls already pricked out waiting to be hardened off in cold frames; but especially when the moon is on the rise, cover these frames with old carpet, sacks or even branches to safeguard weeks of work. If semi-hardy shrubs planted in one's garden have been subject to unex-pected frost damage, spray with a watering can before early morning sunshine strikes unwittingly, and remember to cover them before nightfall with branches or newspaper. I was badly caught last week with newly planted white rhododendrons called 'Everest', thought to be hardily grown. They must have been brought on into glorious flower for the market under glass, although sold as if they had been hard-ened off. A present of beautiful ruby coloured pansies were fortunately put into an open summerhouse, and even they looked chilled. One cannot be too careful when blackthorn gives warning to old-fashioned gardeners.

SEEDLINGS AND WILD FLOWERS

May 1990

To see a world in a grain of sand
And a Heaven in a wild flower

William Blake 1757-1827

In these days when natural herbage is very limited, the grass in many country churchyards fortunately remains uncut until much later in the summer. This provides havens of tranquillity for nesting birds, or food and quiet for butterflies and many small creatures, where they can remain undisturbed for many weeks.

It is indeed fortunate that oases of hospitality remain in these days of modernisation of our countryside, and although meadowland is at last being "set aside", acres have already been deprived of many precious and rare wild flowers through fertilisation and ploughing.

I was sitting in our pew in Dacre Church recently, early one perfect Sunday morning, having left the chancel door opposite, opened wide. A song thrush, perching on an old sand coloured tombstone, wakened the morning with hymns of glory, while a fat wood pigeon sat upon another. Butterflies and bees were plentiful, their wings transparent in May sunlight. A woodpecker drummed on an elm tree down by the beck edge, its pale yellow clusters of flowers a glory to behold. Thank goodness that elm trees still sprout shoots from their stools, and seedling trees grow for many years before they probably fall victim to Dutch Elm disease. Golden elms of Dutch origin appear to grow successfully, their leaves of rich harvest colour. One of these golden elms, planted in the Wild Garden, is much admired by visitors.

We planted out our sweet peas ten days ago on a somewhat hot day, but during the night in the fickle weather of Maytime, much rain fell, and the sweet peas were safely established with Heaven-sent showers. Vegetable seeds, scarcely in the ground, have germinated in the warmed-up soil, and even seeds sown in the glass-house appear so quickly that one must remember to remove shading newspaper and then plastic covers or glass. A good tip is to scatter or riddle a little fine soil mix over newly germinated primula and other seedlings to give these fragile youngsters the protection they need against the sun. This is most effective among delphinium seedlings which rapidly become leggy.

Sadly, Barnhaven Nurseries at Brigsteer are giving up at the end of the season, so this year and last, we have grown a quantity of their seed. One of my treasures is *Primula sieboldii* which I call "The Chinese Primula"; its small, clear white and lilac-pink flower heads grow six inches above toothed leaves, its colouring reminding one of delicate Chinese porcelain. Fortunately it sets some seedlings and forms offshoots in our gardens and at this time of year small clusters of established seedlings are easily transplanted in rich moist soil. *Primula alpicola violacea* with deep violet-blue drooping heads, heavily coated with farina, are filled with the most mysteriously wonderful perfume. They too, need cool, semi-shade; in warm June evenings the air is filled with their fragrance. Its close relative in this *sikkimensis* group, *P. alpicola luna,* the moonlight primula, is of the most subtle, beautiful sulphur yellow, its stems also only 30 cm tall. These primulas seed easily in the right conditions and multiply so that they divide readily.

In the midst of busy gardening activities I promised myself to take time off and look for wild flowers known to be growing on primaeval ground, where limestone escarpments create little valleys and hills throughout a splendid grazing ground for young cattle. On reaching the highest point, the flattish, north-facing rocks were a picture — alive with tiny cranesbills, and in grassy patches early purple orchis with spotted leaves, grew everywhere. I knelt on the ground to photograph, with a herd of inquisitive, hand-reared stirks licking my jacket: they liked the company and moved quietly wherever I walked. My evening was "made" when one small patch of meadow saxifrage came into view, their white, five-petalled flowers streaked with delicate green lines. This *saxifraga granulata* was once common in Cumbrian meadows. The end of the park at Dalemain, always laid up for hay to be mown with a pair of Clydesdale horses, was their home. It was one of my childhood delights to find their starry flowers in early summertime. Now they are a rarity.

High up on the southern aspects of the escarpments, thousands of dandelion clocks shone with evening sunlight, while cowslips flourished on soft grass below. My Mother sometimes said, "Memories are happiness." I shall never forget this Sunday evening amongst precious wild flowers.

SECRET PLACES

This is the place where I'd love to lie
Where hilltops meet with a wandering sky;
Where winter storms and the sunbeams meet
When spring returns, then the fells are sweet
Waters rise up from a world below,
Life giving springs, rich with blanketing snow.

Small hidden treasures awake round my tread,
Red rosy orchids in soft grassy bed
Butterfly orchids like pure clotted cream
Primrose and butterwort wake by the stream
Sun dazzled king cups and marsh marigold
Arise from the rushes, their glories unfold.

Magical music I hear everywhere
Small birds in the sunshine — larks in the air
This is my Heaven, their song shall I sing,
As I follow the valley to go to my King.

1989

THE PARADISIACAL WORLD OF
WILD FLOWERS

June 1987

Have the wild flowers been particularly beautiful this year, or do we see them with "new eyes" at every season? If we are acutely aware of the world outside, every new shape and colour fills our vision, even momentarily, as we pass along familiar paths; winds rustle mysteriously, among graceful grasses, or sing soothingly among triangular-stemmed sedges. The countryside is bounteously beautiful.

Do many people realise that there are nearly four hundred different species of the rubus family alone, varying from enchanting golden-faced tormentils that flourish on dry natural banks, to tall stately verbascums whose colours vary from clover through shades of pinks and whites; or purple headed burnets whose added glory is their deeply segmented grey-green foliage; or meadowsweets that fill our meadow-lands with delicious scent — on and on goes the list, through prickly brambles and many others, to several varieties of wild roses which sprawl and scramble over everything that acts as support at this present season.

The Lake District is particularly fortunate in its wide variety of flowers and grasses, which have evolved with archaeological upheavals and transformations of our fells and dales; even more important, plant life has evolved with the unseen threadwork of springs and secret watercourses. Carboniferous limestone formations produce an entirely different vegetation to the volcanic central masses around Skiddaw: rich alluvial valley bottoms, fed by countless chattering becks frequently laden with peat from primaeval forests, grow valerians, water forget-me-nots, burnets and wild orchids which are a joy to every botaniser's heart. Their season of colour is not long, but when growing in remote wilds which see no hay machines nor fertiliser, they seed at will.

The orchid family, Orchidaceae is large and varied, this ancient Greek name possibly referring to the two oblong tubers at the root. Many species including helleborines, which grow in woods of beech, oak and ash, boggy places or even dry grassy places, are but a few of their number: but proud and colourful early purple orchis is the species I have known and loved since I was a very small child, so easily found in woodlands not far from Dalemain. It was in these woodlands that I made one of my many little gardens, because these purple orchids grew amongst beech trees woodsorrel and windflowers.

On higher marginal land known as the Divisions, father's herd of Galloway cattle ran with the white Shorthorn bull all summer. Margaret and I rode with him on our ponies to shepherd the cattle and sheep on this unspoilt moor.

Here we found so many wild flowers; the graceful butterfly orchid, its vanilla scented, creamy-white flowers carried above a single pair of elliptical, shining leaves was the flower we easily searched for while Father looked carefully at the black cows with their followers. On this ground, spotted, sweet-scented and marsh orchids all grew, and best of all, *Primula farinosa*, the small Bird's Eye Primrose, its lilac-pink flowers with yellow eyes held together in an umbrella above a rosette of pale green leaves. These grew in open damp places above the retreats of marsh loving flowers.

These, and many more, were carefully gathered — only one specimen of each species because it was instilled into us from early days that wild flowers must be encouraged to reproduce themselves. These treasures were taken indoors, painted carefully in drawing books, and then pressed between newspaper upon which a few heavy books were laid for a week or so. I still have my early collection in photograph albums, which became final resting places for pressed flowers of many sorts.

My deep love of flowers was inherited from forbears whose deep love of the land was intentionally passed on to succeeding generations. Grandfather, Canon George Hasell, loved children and understood country matters. He continued to live at Dalemain with us all until he died in 1932, for Granny died in 1919, the year before our parents were married. I was always ready to go with him across the fields or by the river edge. We'd find cuckoo flowers along the ditch below Park

House, nodding their lilac-pink flowers while their hawk-like namesakes proclaimed the nesting season from solitary outposts not far away. "Those flowers are also called Our Lady's Smock," said dear Grandfather, reverently, as we laid our finds carefully in the wicker basket he always carried; those salmon-red water avens — *Geum rivale* — are Soldiers' buttonholes, remembering soldiers of the far-flung British Empire.

One of these wicker baskets was Grandfather's "acorn basket". As a child, he and his Nanny constantly gathered acorns, which they sowed broadcast in the Evening Bank, the wood situated on the limestone ridge at the top of the park above the farm buildings. These acorns grew freely to become a fine stand of timber, thinned many years later by my father.

Along the whole length of the park, this bank of rough limestone extended with its strange organ-like pipes forming a barrier with fields above, a wood of handsome trees has grown since it was replanted in 1946-47: Scots firs on the uppermost acres and mainly beech below, and still this splendid crop of oaks clothing the Evening Bank. Beneath the canopy of trees primroses and violets scent the air with fragrance and in their place bluebells, those wild hyacinths of woodlands create carpets as blue as summer skies which they truly reflect at this season of the year.

The eighteenth-century planting of beech and oak was sadly felled in 1940, when our islands became the bastion of freedom against a terrifying aggressor, but, as usual, nature laid her carpet of wild flowers to cover the destruction of tree felling. Wild strawberries grew everywhere on this sun-warmed bank; baskets full of these ruby delicacies were gathered. Wild garlic or ramsons always grew in profusion which Shorthorn cattle ate greedily at "turning out" time: this medicinal herb provided an essential tonic for their well-being, despite our milk tasting of the stuff; everyone grumbled but the human race will always grumble when the chance occurs. The wealth of strawberries have long since gone into hibernation, until "the next cut".

I constantly feel I owe a deep debt of gratitude to Etta Murray, who came to Dalemain as governess to my sister, Margaret, and myself when I was eight years old and she was five. Etta's father, Robert Murray, and his father and grandfather before, farmed Low Plains near Calthwaite and were each highly thought-of yeomen farmers. Her mother was the first District Nurse in that area, arriving by train at Calthwaite station for her first job where she was met by Mrs Harris of Brackenbrough Tower who was president of Cumberland's Nursing Association. Mrs Harris was a very beautiful and elegant lady, and together they drove off to inspect a little of the new District in a carriage drawn by a pair of smart horses. In the years that followed, until her marriage, Mrs Murray looked after her district, travelling her rounds on a bicycle, unless some kind farmer or landowner offered a welcome ride in varying horse-drawn vehicles. In this way she cared for sick people and small children throughout a wide area, with the added anxiety and delight of bringing new babies into this slow-moving, old-fashioned world of hayfields, Shorthorn cattle and Clydesdale horses.

Etta was educated at Carlisle High School for girls, where a wonderful teacher of like-minded qualities, Miss Routledge, if my memory is correct, taught her the elements of botany. Thereafter she arrived at Dalemain to look after us and lay the foundations of an education based on the miracles of the countryside. In her trunk came the Rev John's *Flowers of the Field*, now a highly recognised work.

We were brought up on this illustrated volume and upon Bentham & Hooker's *British Flora* from Father's bookshelves; these bookshelves were otherwise mainly concerned with treatises on agriculture and forestry and of his days at Oxford as a pupil of Sir William Somerville and later as his student assistant. Sir William, who was born at Cormiston, an attractive farmhouse overlooking the Clyde at Quothquan, held the first ever Chair of Agriculture, first at Durham, then at Cambridge, and finally at Oxford. Sir William and my equally keen father began their experiments in Poverty Bottom which was the most dreadfully poor land near Oxford. This land was transformed by experimenting with basic slag.

WILLOW WREN

I'd love to be a willow wren
Beside a moving stream,
Where tasselled catkins hang and blow
Rejoice in springtime's dream.

I'd love to be a willow wren
Soprano notes she'll sing,
Well hid in tangled undergrowth
Rejoicing with the spring.

I'd love to watch a willow wren
Just hear her sweet refrain
Stand, listen, to her magic voice —
I hear her yet again.

1990

WONDERS OF THE WAYSIDE

June 1987

How fortunate we are to live in Cumbria, especially at this season of the year, for this unique corner of the British Isles is particularly rich in its flora. We may grumble at the weather, but if it were not for an abundant rainfall, many of these treasures — and some are truly rarities — would not survive in drier, hotter conditions.

Roadside verges and laybys are usually a haven for wild flowers; it is sad and unnecessary for these untrammelled waysides to be sprayed or cut. It is not only plant life that thrives in untrodden areas; they are a haven for wild life, including many sorts of butterflies and moths. How sad it would be if our children and grandchildren grew up without understanding the glories of red admiral and peacock butterflies.

I read that there are about 171,000 acres of road verges in Britain, and since these acres are of no use for agricultural purposes we must each do our best to conserve them for the heritage of flora and fauna. May 16-25 1987 was National Wild Flower week, but in every week throughout the year we must promote this cause and teach our children to follow in our footsteps.

May and June are the season of particularly beautiful wild flowers. The graceful grass of Parnassus, its white, buttercup-like flowers veined with grey, smelling faintly of honey, pervades marshy ground and secret places among our fells; here, too, deep blue butterworts with rosettes of shining, buttermilk-like leaves grow, and frequently wild orchids — purple, marsh, and fragrant white butterfly varieties: these live in harmony with twayblades and those enchanting Birds' Eye Primroses (*Primula farinosa*) whose lilac faces and mealy farina are a joy to behold, especially when one comes upon such treasures unexpectedly.

We often went up into Martindale with Father when he intended to see about some farming matter at Thrangcrag. This peaceful valley was always my dream-world. Its dark, mysterious water courses were full of fascination, for their rushy verges were, and still are, a paradise for flowers — marsh marigolds, burnets, scabious and those beautiful pink cuckoo flowers. Brown trout were numerous, sailing around in quieter pools, almost mesmerizing to watch as they swam this way and that, or leaped to catch midges and flies.

When Etta Murray arrived at Dalemain, she was able to teach us the little things that really matter in the lives of country children. Etta's copy of the Rev John's "Flowers of the Field" became our bible of the countryside. Many a day we searched for flowers, even on sunlit wintery days when rare toothworts, those orchid-like parasites, flowered at the roots of lime and elm trees near the roadside in the park, or the tiny green moschatel caught our eyes on a woodland bank where first primroses and violets flourished faithfully year by year. One never forgets these dreamlike days of childhood.

Not long ago I came upon one of those old fashioned side roads, probably a Roman road, with wide verges, these margins essential in days when highwaymen might lurk in wait to plunder horsedrawn carriages. It was a warm June day and these verges were glowing with sweetly scented pale pink, spotted orchis; not far away Blencathra's substantial summits, partially hidden with sunlit morning mists, created an atmosphere of peace, timelessness and harmony.

Why not encourage wild flowers to grow in a corner of your garden? So easy and so rewarding. Watch for seeds of your favourites to become ripe, and only then, gather some — there is no need to pull up the parent plant — nature is very generous. Sow the desired seed in open ground, or in a wooden box, and leave this out of doors in a sheltered, but not too dry corner. After sowing the seed, scatter the used flower heads beside the seed to remind you, in case labels should be lost. Two years ago, I sowed the most beautiful of the great Umbellifer family, Sweet Cicely, and now in our garden, it is a joy to behold. In a patch of unmown grass, bluebells, scabious, campions and all manner of flowers can grow to follow each other throughout the season: while fritillaries, crocus and other little bulbs, or even martagon lilies can be naturalised to emerge in even greater numbers when spring unfailingly returns. Lift up your hearts, rejoice and be glad, for our wild flowers are as stars of the morning skies.

ASCENSION DAY

How often on Ascension Day
The sky is clear, and always blue,
As Heaven shines upon our Earth
With powerful irridescent hue.
Far up above, where skylarks sing
Our church bells resonantly ring.

That lovely sound that carries far
Across fresh fields of greening grain,
They peal from every fellside tower
Their peal of praise repeats again,
While city churches call to pray
Because it is Ascension Day.

Our family, with our ponies, climbed
The highest fellside of them all;
Sweet Blossoms, long lost from our views,
We, on Helvellyn's ridge, felt small.
Ascendingly, we rode that way
To celebrate Ascension Day.

When German war planes bombed and strafed
Our ships, off Alexandria's harboured shore*
Each man must keep his station to the last,
"Valiant" enduring all she could and more;
Her Padre, full of thankful, fearful pride,
Commander Dick so often near his side;
Who, sometimes being a humorous strength and stay
Despite grim horrors of that watery way;
How glad he was to hear Dick softly say,
"Remember this *is* the Lord's Ascension Day!

1991

*It was in 1941 when HMS Valiant took part in this action. She had
lately been the first ship to be fitted with radar, so was much needed as
protection for other ships.

POPPIES FOR REMEMBRANCE

June 1989

Gazing out of our windows in the early hours of a June morning is, as if one is allowed to peep at something of eternal beauty. Lights of dawn breaking steadily across the heavens; pale yellows, rosy pinks, and sea greens sending shafts of glory through woodlands still hushed in slumber. Mists of pearly dawn sparkle on daisies growing upon mown grass between the house and open woodlands; these woodlands — outer fringes of our Wild Garden — provide shelter for maples originating from far-off lands; colourful low growing rhododendrons and glamorous ferns lend an air of mystery.

Dawn lights grow stronger, lighting up the faces of a veritable sea of blue Himalayan poppies, their childlike faces looking outwards, as if in wonder, to be roused at this early hour; for three o'clock in the morning is a never-to-be-forgotten time to be awake at midsummer, when there is time to think, unhurriedly, and to be able to gaze out into the treasure-house of dawn.

Blue poppies belong to my world of dream-like fantasies, especially when sun-beams reflect their brilliance through insubstantial petals; this is particularly true of Cicely Crewdson's meconopsis which is the clearest sky blue of the several species and hybrids known to me. Cicely was a close friend of my grandfather and a frequent visitor at Dalemain when I was a small child; she and grandfather talked about plants while I listened, sitting close beside grandfather, never to forget those moments.

We sat at the round walnut table taking tea: table cloths were fine white linen embroidered with open worked stitching, always freshly laundered. Mother poured out tea from a round Georgian teapot, while a silver kettle brewed fresh hot water above a methylated flame. Mrs Crewdson always wore a rather high hat with a brim, for she was visiting.

The room was filled with all manner of bookcases, for this was Grandfather's library, where he kept "everything" safe: it was always used for tea, for it was warmed, lit up by evening sunlight.

It was so fortunate that I came upon Cicely's meconopsis, quite unexpectedly, when purchasing other plants in Jack Drake's nursery at Aviemore, and noticed a label *Meconopsis crewdsonii*. A strange intuitive feeling awoke long ago happy memories: could they possibly be something to do with Grandfather's old friend? So I bought three plants for the garden at Huntfield and three for Dalemain. They are a constant joy whenever their pointed leaves appear, or when their flowers become luminous in the sunshine.

George Sheriff's wondrously rich blue poppies were my earliest find, forming huge tough clumps of perennial plants with somewhat furry leaves that have a warm red-brown glow in their colouring. George and his friend, Frank Ludlow, first went to Burma and Tibet in 1933 where he found his meconopsis. He must be proud of his wondrous poppies growing with abandon in our acid soil at Huntfield which never dries out, and in rich alluvial soil flooded by Dacre's beck sometimes in the winter.

I was so thankful to find that these much loved flowers would grow easily in both our different gardens with plenty of humus to protect their root system, for where would we be without the romance of their beauty. In other parts of the garden different forms of Himalayan poppies thrive, *M.* x *sheldonii*, *M.* x *S.* 'Slieve Donard', and *M. baileyi*, which was the first of the "blue" poppies to be discovered, each very different to observant gardeners, each with its own ethereal beauty.

Colourful oriental poppies of reds, flame or white, sometimes fringed majestically, have grown in cottage gardens up and down the land for many generations: these belong to another genus, Papaveraceae, and were a symbol of glory and magnificence in Victorian times, bringing interest to herbaceous borders in early weeks of summer.

Shirley poppies, those elegant little flowers of pale pinks and reds and shades of white, have long been bought in packets of seeds by children for their small gardens; yellow Iceland or Welsh poppies grow easily in sunny well-drained sites where their self-sown seedlings rise to replace parent plants for years to come, growing from the most unexpected difficult cracks in stone walls with the utmost reliance. These are the only member of the genus Meconopsis known in the Western Hemisphere.

Best known of all are the tough red field poppies growing profusely in cornfields in drier acres and roadsides of Britain, extending their brilliance far across the English Channel, whose waters have safeguarded the freedom of our islands throughout the centuries.

Harvest fields become brilliant with their upturned faces; it was these poppies that have always clothed the battlefields of Flanders, screening some of the sadness and tragedy that befell these countries. What is so wonderful about these small field poppies? Each plant holds its own resurrection to a new dawning of light and glory in springtime, giving our frail faiths a simple Sunday School lesson of the Truth, for how readily in our own sadnesses we forgot those immortal words, "Consider the lilies of the field, how they grow . . ." We too must have a resurrection if these small flowers can show us the way. Tough little field poppies do not grow in tbe colder, wetter areas of Britain, but in their stead, unfailingly, sunloving meconopsis reflect the blues of early summer skies together with those enduring poppies of Wales, spreading their happiness far afield to gladden our hearts when we are sad.

Little children, who, fortunately, have not known the sadness of much that happened before they were born, gather posies of poppies in many countries to bring laughter to our eyes, and for us these courageous flowers have come to symbolize our remembrance.

Poppies of so many habits, blooming in their own seasons, can teach us much when we are quiet, and can open our hearts and minds to understand. When the busy world is hushed, we can dream and remember.

PETALS OF PERFECTION

June 1990

A party of American gardening enthusiasts came to see our garden at Huntfield in early June. Most of them were from around Boston and they were touring Scottish gardens with their leader Peter Ashton, who was Professor of Botany and Dendrology at that university. He formerly held this post at Aberdeen University and became quite excited to see the many "old" roses growing in our garden. "Look, Mary," he frequently exclaimed to his wife, "those are just like the roses we grew in our garden at Aberdeen."

The old Burnet roses were of particular interest, for many of these originated in little gardens along the East Coast belonging to miners and fishermen. These men frequently had wonderful gardens and in earlier days began to hybridise the native *Rosa spinosissima*, now classified as *Rosa pimpinellifolia*, and seek out preferred mutations of these beautiful little roses. Their small ferny foliage is borne on densely populated stems with needle-like prickles. They sucker freely and grow easily in most soils, particularly on sandy soil, hence their native habitations near the east coast. Simply described as Scots briar roses, they were known in Europe pre-1600, and over the years have given rise to many and varied hybrids, having invariably the most delicious perfume.

Having collected some of these roses over a period of many years, they have grown into handsome thickets, but being most obliging in their suckering habits, pieces were easily moved to Dalemain and other places. Mine have usually been named after the places or people from whence they originated. The old 'Double White' is most beautiful, with small, shining globular almost black hips in autumn. One of the loveliest is the Thankerton Rose, a marbled, clover-coloured Burnet rose which I rescued from a tumbled thatched-roofed railway cottage in this village near Huntfield, its garden rapidly becoming a builders' dumping ground. The fallen roof attracted my attention to collect an additional joy.

On another occasion I spied another Burnet rose that was new to us, on a disused railway embankment near Edinburgh. Persuading Bryce to stop the car for just a moment as we drove our boys back to school in Fife after a happy, but all too short, day with them at home, I jumped out of the car to collect a good suckering piece which came away easily with an urgent tug. These roses are alive with minute thorns along their stems and I have forgotten now, how many were lodged in my fingers, but the rose grew: that was the main thing.

A lovely double yellow briar came from two old Knox cousins, Martha and Jenny, who had the most prolific garden of long standing at Place above Kilbirnie village in north Ayrshire. This form is much less coarse than the woodier 'Harrison's Yellow', also known as the Yellow Rose of Texas. Mine is said to be of very ancient origin.

Yet another, small-flowered double yellow was given to me by Grizel Bertram, an old friend who lived near Innerleithen on a high-lying farm where she bred her Galloway cattle: her present grows as her memorial in our garden.

Primula Sieboldii

The Walled Garden at Huntfield

Spanish Beauty, Dalemain

Lilium Giganteum

The American visitors could scarcely appreciate the size and abundance of our herbaceous plants: the secret is the precious gift of water, combined with friability of well fed soil. *Euphorbia griffithii* 'Fireglow' glows like a burst of sunlight: its deep orange-red flower heads stand up straight to set off neighbourly *Rodgersia pinnata* with large horse-chestnut-shaped, truly ornamental leaves and fluffy, creamy white flowers; but our Himalayan poppies are a glorious introduction to the Meconopsis family for visitors from afar. George Sheriff's deep blue, wide faced, poppy increases all over our gardens.

When I take my little dogs for a walk at dusk, the evening light, so ethereal at this hour, filters through an enormous rowan in full flower, satisfactorily placed behind a bank of varying rhododendrons. In front of all these magical sleepy colours grows a wide bank of blue poppies. The whole effect is something almost unbelievably wonderful.

Tree peonies are coming to their best at this time of year, their leaves ornamental in any garden, in addition to their "thousand-petalled" flowers by which name the Chinese referred to their peonies. They were widely gown in northern China as early as 600 AD, grown notably for their beauty, but in addition the root of the Mudan or Moutan, the tree peony, was prescribed in ancient herbals for high blood pressure.

Tree peonies are not difficult to grow in almost any kind of soil; the graft must be below soil level when planted, so that the plant soon acquires its own roots. The site should be well manured wth compost and in addition, an annual dressing of bone meal. Some tree peonies are no taller than herbaceous peonies. *P.* 'Chromatella' is pale sulphur yellow tinged with pink and always causes interest in our garden. Deep rose pink *P.* 'Duchess of Marlborough' is just beginning to flower, for they take a few years to become truly established, but it is well worth waiting for their lasting beauty.

Peonies enjoy horse or cow manure, and once planted, with their crowns not more than two inches below the surface, they must remain undisturbed in order to flower profusely. Their sweetly scented blooms make long lasting cut flowers. Peonies are immune to attacks by rabbits which is frequently a great asset. I must make room for several "new" peonies to be planted in our two gardens when autumn returns, all too quickly. 'Shirley Temple' is one of these, its profuse soft pink flowers fading almost to white with a marvellous glow within its broad outer petals.

FOR LOVE OF A ROSE

Rambling roses, tumble blow
Where precious alpine treasures grow;
Roses, yellow, pink and red
Spilling from their gravelled bed.

Rambling over ancient walls
Where joyously the blackbird calls;
Walls below this old grey pele
When wars and siege were very real.

With flowers these walls were later dress'd
Whose scented joys were much caressed;
With lavender and lilies too,
Sweet herbs to catch the morning dew.

The sun may shine and winter cold
But rambling roses firmly hold;
For roses are this garden's Queen,
The best of all, old Albertine.

March 1988

COLLECTING "OLD" ROSES

July 1987

> "I'll say she looks as clear as morning roses,
> newly washed with dew."

In William Shakespeare's 'Taming of the Shrew' he writes these words which alone speak of the inherent love of most precious flowers known and cultivated from earliest times. They were depicted on the finest Chinese porcelain and stitched frequently in Persian tapestries, and painted on their sculpture.

It was from Persia and China that so many of our species roses originated, and from their parentage many of our present-day roses are bred. *Rosa gallica* was cultivated by the Medes and Persians as early as the 12th century B.C. and was revered by them as a religious symbol; it was grown by the ancient Greeks in Asia Minor, from whence the Romans imported it, although it is considered native as far flung as Persia to France. This gallica, known also *as Rosa rubra*, or red rose, was one of the parents of so many Damask roses, and the lovely and most important *R. gallica officinalis*, the Apothecary's Rose, with its large, semi-double crimson flowers which open wide to display its golden stamens, scenting the air with delicious fragrance: it was a source of medicine and healing, later to become the emblem of the Lancastrians during the Wars of the Roses.

Rosa canina, the wild dog rose found in hedges in many countries of Europe, is the parent of many ancient roses, including, probably, *R. alba* and her large family. She was thought to be the emblem of the Virgin, during the Middle Ages. The history and love of the rose is endless, being so often the symbol of frequent historical associations such as the white rose of York, the red rose of Lancaster; while Bonnie Prince Charlie's *R. Alba Maxima*, another species of antiquity, its double white flowers flushed at the centre with cream, became the emblem of the Young Pretender and his followers.

Every garden grows a rose of some sort; small gardens frequently grow a climbing variety which may be pruned in autumn to decorate its walls, while other rambling roses are allowed to scramble as a hedge along the fence giving passers-by enormous pleasure, for it is their fragrance which delights the senses. Roses make wonderful hedges as we can understand from the use of our wild dog rose clipped into shape by farmers who long understood its usefulness in keeping sheep and rough cattle in their allotted pastures.

In our own gardens, *R. farreri persetosa*, the Threepenny Bit Rose, is my favourite of this type, so called for its tiny pink flowers. It may be lightly clipped as a hedge or used as a semi-procumbent shrub, its arching hairy branches covered with tiny fern-like leaves which turn purple and crimson in autumn. It is just as beautiful in winter when sunlight mirrors through sparkling frost settling on these branches each covered in minute hairy thorns. It is a rose which enjoys partial shade. One grown as a cutting and planted beside the Wendy House in the Wild Garden has grown into a truly ornamental bush. 'Celestial' is perhaps the most perfect of all, of Eastern origin and of very ancient parentage. It is extremely easy to grow since it increases by suckering on its own roots, soon creating a small family of healthy, semi double soft pink flowers with exotic perfume; its grey-green foliage is unmistakable in any garden. I found this rose, previously unknown to me, growing in our garden at Brownhill, our Ayrshire home, soon after the war. "It's just one of those Ayrshire roses", I was constantly told, for this part of the country was well known for "its" roses, usually nameless. 'Celestial' is one of the earliest to bloom, with a very long flowering season.

Old roses that will climb and scramble through the branches of trees can be very lovely. *Rosa moschata* 'Floribunda' is magnificent when its clusters of creamy-white flowers climb among dark yew branches or when they make a picture fanned out on a sunny wall. Each primrose-like flower has a ring of yellow stamens, its fragrance wonderful. It also hangs over the Wild Garden wall so that some of its branches can be safely tied on to a blanket of ivy.

There are many good worthwhile shrub roses. David Austin produced his English roses, some of which are very beautiful, and frequently recurrent flowering. A rich yellow in the tradition of Old Roses with a strong fragrance is named after one the great gardeners and writers of present times, Graham Thomas. Heritage is a lovely, scented pink and perfect form. Several of these similarly bred roses have grown for some years in our gardens. It is important to try out a few of the best modern roses to keep one's collection up to date; one cannot live only in the past.

Although my two gardens are so full of shrub roses, there is always room to squeeze in perhaps one more forgotten treasure.

HERBACEOUS BORDERS IN SUMMERTIME

July 1989

At this time of year, worthwhile seedlings of many kinds have germinated amongst our plants, and while one weeds, one's eyes must be constantly aware of seedlings which are well worth preserving: strangers may be carried in by wind or insects, and one must be ever alert to forms and colours one does not expect to find. If ground is dry these treasures should be marked, as they are probably safer where they have taken root than moved to seed beds, until later. Occasionally seedlings of our seventeenth century Grecian silver fir emerge in boxwood hedges, and as these are rare in Britain, they must be transferred later to a seedbed into which leafmould is incorporated, and grown on; seedlings of that useful shrub rose *R. rubrifolia*, with its magnificent crop of dark red berries spring up, and like smaller plants, enjoy conditions near gravelled paths where drainage is perfect.

Exhaustive dry weather in June caused one to think of which plants survive best in these conditions. Our Terrace border of herbaceous plants is liable to be battered by winter storms and icy cold weather in winter or baked with sunshine in summer so that during the winter plants must be coated with plenty of farm manure which will break down into rich humus, encouraging them to draw their moisture far below the surface in times of drought. Bearded iris are ideal for our border, since their tubers require to be baked to bring them into flower. *Crambe cordate* with massive long stemmed gypsophila-like flowers and impressive glossy foliage, is always an ornamental addition; old fashioned Goat's Beard, *Aruncus plumosus*, produces erect plumes of creamy-white good foliage for sheltering less fortunate neighbours which benefit from some shade. Silver and variegated plants enjoy sunshine. Artemisias both large and small, pineapple mint and *Symphytum peregrinum*, a magnificent type of variegated borage, are admired by everyone. Geraniums and pelargoniums, requiring a holiday, will grow twice as profusely if planted out of doors, but do remember to take cuttings or lift plants before frosts arrive unexpectedly.

Many smaller plants such as alyssum and candytuft seed regularly on the edge of such borders, while forget-me-nots leave many seedlings for another springtime, causing no trouble to anyone. Verbascums, those stately mulleins, spring up in strange places; even on the front of our border they look unexpectedly good, while salvias of several varieties grow well, their name meaning "safe" or "unharmed" in Latin, referring to medicinal properties. Two years ago I sowed *S. forsskaollii* which has long spires of striking deep blue, white-throated flowers with expansive foliage; now large plants, they are a most successful addition to the Terrace border, their wide leaves keeping ground cool beneath their spread.

Phygelius capensis, Cape figwort, with flame-coloured tubular flowers, makes a wonderful show against a warm wall. It is not a true climber but benefits from these conditions. It grew in the walled garden at Huntfield before we bought the estate in 1958. Never having seen the plant before, it has been an exciting colourful asset in both our gardens, and in others too, all over the country when we have had some to spare. Semi-evergreen, a sub-shrub, it sends up new shoots from its base, but when plants have become woody, they can be easily pruned back to live wood when necessary. It is a splendidly colourful and unusual member of the Scrophulariaceae family to exhibit at local Flower Shows.

Clematis have become one of my favourite plants, but of course require opposite conditions to the foregoing. Roots and lower stems must be planted in cool or even dimly lit places, or protected by leafy neighbours. They soon scramble upwards to meet the sunshine. I was advised by a friend to plant further clematis through draining tiles to prevent slugs ruining so many new additions. The lower part of their stems should be planted fully two inches below the surface, so that if slugs do their worst further stems may grow. Drainage tiles pushed down a little into soil around the topmost root areas give added protection. Disused tins would do equally well; it really is a good idea. One is continually learning something new in the world outside.

EVENTIDE

Returning homeward, tired, distressed,
Long shadows fill the sunlit skies;
Whene're I reach the beech wood trees
'Tis then my heart begins to rise.
Those dreaming beech boughs bending low
Hide moss and little things below.

October's sunset dazzles clear
Beyond quiet reaches of our hills
I hear the songs of quiet'ning birds
Their melodies rejoice, and fill
My voice with song once truly bleak
Now gently raindrops wash my cheek.

For in these depths a casket hid,
Filled with most precious woodland gems
Hid from the world of noise and dust
Those tiny flowers on fragile stems
Drops of diamonds and pearl-like dew,
Mosses like ferns of silvered blue.

Woods with their own cathedral choir
Singing such sweet magnificat,
Bird choristers at evensong
Bid me to join their hidden chat
With them my song to Heaven will raise
Their sunlit song of priceless praise.

REFLECTION BEFORE PLANTING

July 1989

"Each Morn a thousand Roses bring, you'll say;
Yes, but where leaves the Rose of Yesterday."

How true these words ring in our ears during unusually long weeks of scorching sunshine and lack of rain. Probably such a summer occurred during the first half of the nineteenth century when Edward Fitzgerald wrote these lines in his long remembered "Omar Khayyam."

Both our gardens are filled with roses, more magnificent in stature and in quality and quantity than I can ever recall. But, in so many sunbaked corners of our gardens the rose of yesterday is but a memory of glory. One of my favourite climbers is the dark velvety H. Tea 'Guinée', its petals as lustrous velvet adorning the high Terrace wall, its fragrance perfect; but next day it is a faded beauty. This summer instils into our minds the need to protect and prepare plants for adverse conditions whether it be heat or cold. We plant these treasures where we will, *not* where they would grow if they were given the choice, and so they must be cherished. Wherever possible clothe their roots with rotted strawy manure, leafmould or peat in the autumn; encourage them to burrow deeply with their own roots to those lower regions of the good earth where they will invariably find moisture. Artificial manures will act as tonics, given in their correct seasons, but they have no body to form protective barriers against the elements; it is nature's gifts which do the most good. Some of my primulas which enjoy cool conditions have developed that horrible affliction "fascination": although these plants, particularly the glorious candelabra, alpicola violacae, are planted in normally damp parts of the garden, abnormal conditions have caused a number of stems to fuse side by side, forming a broad, flat, leathery ribbon-like stem: some of the flowers have also acquired an irregular fusion. Normally their slim, elegant stems carry misty, lilac flowers each coated with farina, their perfume in the cool of the evening more glamorous than the most expensive French scent.

In Huntfield's cool, peaty soil, the drought has scarcely affected them. Here roses and other flowers have really bloomed, which usually struggle to make a show. Ferdinand Pichard is a marvellous repeat flowering striped shrub rose to plant in the autumn. Marketed in 1910, it grows about three feet tall and as wide, spreading itself most beautifully to create an eye-catching appearance. *Rosa gallica* versicolor was perhaps the earliest known striped rose, said to have been brought home to England by the Crusaders in the twelfth century. This was about the same time that moated towers and castles were built in various parts of the country including Dacre Castle: it is absolutely amazing how these fortresses were built to stand so many centuries. It is even more wonderful that a small shrub rose, carried home among some Crusader's baggage all the way from the Middle East, for his lady, should have survived for us to look upon.

It was such a novelty to have a striped rose, something entirely new, and the King, Henry II, called one of these *Rosa mundi* after his mistress Fair Rosamund.

Plants that have historical associations are always intriguing, not least this beautiful low growing rose of legendary fame, classed amongst Gallicas.

If you have room for a large and magnificent rose, try 'Cerise Bouquet' whose strong thorny branches are wreathed with flowers and splendid foliage; only produced in 1962, she has grown in a fairly dry border shaded by yew trees where fretted sunlight causes her flowers to glow. It is important to use lower growing plants as ground cover, and under Cerise Bouquet's wide expanse, violets, the Victorian fragrant 'Princess of Wales' variety, will be planted liberally in October: they will benefit from farm manure scattered amongst their foliage to feed the rose, and this in turn will protect violet flowers from the elements.

Roots and lower stems of clematis need to be grown in cool conditions and these will thrive when grown amongst tall plants and shrubs. They too like manure, but beware of slugs. Whenever new clematis are planted, their stems are carefully drawn up through a drainpipe or tree guard cut to a third of its size; these guards are pushed a few inches below the surface of the earth where slugs dwell: leaf mould and soil are trickled around the newly planted clematis. Besides affording shelter, such protections really have been a good idea, but remember to water in dry weather. Clematis enjoy growing on sunless walls where they can scramble up towards the light. If they are planted about six inches beneath the ground and their stems do become destroyed, there is a good chance that they will sprout again.

Whenever you plant perennials, try to understand where your new acquisitions would grow in the wild; these thoughts will help to make your plants grow more happily. Euphorbias of many varieties grow in the Middle East; they are conditioned to drier circumstances, as are cactus types of plants. Variegated plants need sunshine to give of their best, but not all enjoy a lack of moisture, particularly *Brunnera maccrophylla* with its ornamental cream and green leaves. This modern blue-eyed Mary certainly brings her garden-party dress to ornament any border in summertime.

Abraham Cowley wrote the following words in the early seventeenth century which I hope will apply to our own gardens in time of drought:

> "The thirsty earth soaks up the rain,
> And drinks and gapes for drink again.
> The plants suck in the earth, and are
> With constant drinking fresh and fair."

HIDDEN PATHWAY

Rich red flagstones line the pathway
Borders edged with sandstone too;
Paths once trod by timeless gard'ners
Where fragile stovehouses seedlings grew.

Heated walls for early fruit buds,
Apricot from far-off lands;
Redbrick walls bore choicest cherries
Where now my snake-barked maple stands.

Cast exotic days behind us
Carefree foliage fills their place.
Painted bright with autumn's fancy
Stitched like ladies gowns of lace.

Ancient rose from farthest China
Reaches up to meet the sky.
Scatters wide her golden tresses
Shelters treasures, frost-prone, shy.

Feathered goatsbeard, scented violets,
Figworts brought from Table Bay
Fill this secret half-hid garden
Sunkissed on each summer's day.

Nothing wasted, nothing daunted
Foliage plants fill shadowed stage
Priceless plants from far-off countries
Gardens stretch from age to age.

March 1988

MIDSUMMER'S MAGIC

July 1989

July is a month of fulfilment, and thus of contentment. Gardens are at the height of perfection; hard work accomplished in previous months has brought the world of nature to perfection. At last we can relax, a little, and revel in the beauty of midsummer — so long as we have remembered to stake precious herbaceous plants that need support and sow a few biennial and perennial seeds which will enhance our gardens in seasons not far ahead.

The night of Friday July 11th brought two inches of rainfall after a spell of wonderful sunshine. Delphiniums were more beautiful and taller than they had been for many years, some ten feet high, in our gardens, and not all of these were protected by walls. Rings of square mesh fencing wire is a wonderfully easy method of staking, so long as they are put over the plants in good time, preferably with one or two taller stout stakes to hold these in place, and to which a ring of string can be added as plants grow. These wire rings are simply removed in the back-end and stored. Farm manure is the only fertiliser most of our plants are given, which encourages bacteria to work and re-invigorate the soil. The Terrace border, created upon the remains of the defences of Dalemain's medieval tower, dries out easily in a hot summer, but the annual winter mulch has done its job and even the vulnerable plants with which drought easily plays havoc, have played their part admirably, covering this herbaceous border in glory.

'Bridesmaid' is one of the most perfect delphiniums to grow, its lilac-blue double flowers breathtakingly beautiful beside other gentian blue varieties. 'Pink Ruffles' with double, compact spires, is an attractive newcomer, and 'Strawberry Fair' even more lovely.

It is not too late to sow a packet of delphinium seed to produce strong young plants which may be lined out next spring. Blackmore and Langdon's excellent seed are well worth growing. Many seeds, such as those interesting varieties of salvia, campanula and pyrethrum, prefer to germinate in darkness. A little while ago I sowed some of these in a shaded cold frame, watered them well, covering them with thick fertilizer bags weighted safely in case of unexpected winds; these seeds needed no further watering and are now safely "through" and attempting to grow on. Other seeds, such as primulas of various species, like to be sown in May/June, probably in wooden boxes which can be watered and left undisturbed in a cool shady part of the garden; they may not even germinate till the following spring. Last year I gathered seed of candelabra primulas, including the fragrant *P. helodoxa* of the Sikkimensis group which grows easily at Huntfield, and the candelabra *P. florindae*, the giant yellow cowslip, whenever their seed pods were ripe. These seeds were sown immediately on top of friable, home-made compost of a somewhat acid nature, watered in to settle, and their containers set behind a sheltered, shady wall. This spring, thousands of seeds germinated and are now being pricked out, even in tiny groups when time allows. They had even spilt over with their bounty and germinated in the path around their boxes. Other seeds sown in the same way a year ago have germinated; hybrids such as the brilliant flame coloured 'Inverewe' cannot set seed, but multiply, and can be divided. One becomes really excited to discover the rebirth of forgotten treasures.

Roses have surpassed themselves in glory this year. Shrub and species roses are much longer lived and more reliable than modern tea roses, their scents are unforgettable, particularly in early morning or in evenings when the world is hushed, and only the excited chatter of baby birds waiting for their evening meal breaks the stillness. Goldfinches wintered safely in the great Grecian silver fir planted as a feature at the far end of the Terrace about 1690. This rare tree is alive with young goldfinches, while every other bush or hedge is a secret home for other guests. The greatest joy are swallows who have made their home in my potting shed, for as long as I can remember. They are fascinating birds for a child to watch, flying in and out through their own particular entrances. Baby swallows never seem to be satisfied with their last meal. Long may they bring luck and tidings of happiness, rearing their young in the safety of my potting shed. Kingfishers nested above Dacre's Beck beside the Wild Garden for countless years, but are sadly missing of late. Their brilliance was one of my childhood joys. Too much seepage from silage pits or from slurry find their way into the little streams and thence into the becks nowadays, killing much life in the waters, and the foods of birds like those colourful fishermen.

FRESH ENCOUNTERS

July 1990

It was fascinating to explore another part of England's varied countryside throughout our few days' holiday in early July. Shropshire's narrow, high-banked roads on Wenlock Edge were the most beautiful, but where we hoped we would not meet any on-coming traffic. Quiet, idyllic places as they must have been hundreds of years ago; tree branches meeting above our heads; undergrowth that gives little creatures safe shelter.

Part of Gloucestershire horrified us with fields "set aside", no longer used for agricultural purposes; huge thistles rampant, or last year's wheat seed struggling to hold on. That this important, rich part of the country should allow such management seemed quite unrealistic. Alongside such malpractices, picturesque villages were filled with flowers and good ornamental trees; hollyhock-lined pavements, growing and reseeding into the merest crevices. Fortunately we sowed a packet of hollyhock seed in the spring and these have been individually potted and some already planted in permanent quarters where space allows. There is still time to sow a panful, and overwinter the seedlings with protection. They always remind me of childhood stories of "Amelia Anne" and the little village shop where hollyhocks grew sedately beside every house along the village street.

In Chipping Campden a very beautiful and elegant, medium tree caught our eyes. Its seedpods were laburnum-like hanging from intensely green barked branches; the maple-like leaves had cream margins which looked like butterflies as sunlight gave them an ethereal quality. This turned out to be *Acer negundo* 'Variegatum', and although it dislikes east winds, I intend to plant one in a sheltered place. There is also a medium-sized shrub, *Acer palmatum* 'Butterfly', its coral pink young leaves becoming green with cream edges which should be beautiful, though expensive, as are most of the ornamentals. If they can be protected with plastic netting or fine branches till they are truly established, one can only conclude what marvellous Christmas presents have been planted in one's garden.

The Flower Show at the Royal was well worth a visit. The huge marquee was filled to capacity. Roses were predominant. Many were old plant friends, still to the fore. Both Gregory of Stapleford, Nottingham, and Fryer's of Knutsford, Cheshire, produced *R.* 'Margaret Merrill', their sweetest scented rose which they have grown for many years: white overlaid with satin pink, this Floribunda looks perfect in shadowed sunlight. I was very taken with Fryer's short growing Floribundas; their spectacular 'Regensburg' was a mass of flowers in clusters, rich pink with a white eye, and yellow daisy-like centres. 'Deb's Delight', a fragrant salmon pink, is another useful addition with which to edge a border. Small-faced violas grown as a carpet beneath roses will give so much additional pleasure.

Lilies scented the marquee. These are lovely grown three to a 9-inch pot with plenty of leaf mould and sharp sand and a little bone meal. Feed occasionally with phostegen or blood, fish and bone. When they become somewhat pot bound plant the whole pot-ful into your garden and start a new collection of lilies to stand in a sheltered corner or beside a pool. Scatter slug pellets round those grown in the soil. Blackmore and Langdon's delphiniums were, as usual, magnificent. Grow a packet of their seed, and prick them out into a shady frame where you can look after them, feed and water and protect from slugs until they are eighteen months old and strong plants. I was pricking out strongly rooted white seedlings an hour before midnight in mid July: the evening was perfect, cool and fly proof, and the garden like a dream world in a hot summer's dusk, but already, darkness falls considerably earlier than at midsummer.

We chased around the marqee for a pale pink, double fuchsia, 'Southgate', which we grew years ago, and found it among one of several fuchsia displays, so brought home about five different little plants, as well as yet more rock plants and other little treasures.

Travelling on to Hereford, we saw the wonderfully carved Norman cathedral, and the magnificent bridge over the River Wye. This was built by an able Bishop in the early 13th century who was also Keeper of the King's Seals. The perfection of the tracery of the Cathedral's east window was quite amazing: the brilliant workmanship of constructing such a building so very long ago, together with the perfectly proportioned bridge, still carrying heavy traffic, must never be allowed to fall into disrepair.

So on home: the further north we went the better cultivated and stocked were the fields. No "setting aside" here, where land is valuable and money hard to come by. As we climbed up Shap, with its gentle, grazing sheep, we both felt how lucky we are to live in our wild beautiful north country.

FOR DAVID

Our First Born Grandchild

David, now you're ten years old
I would wish your dreams unfold:
Wishes that you grow up true
And live the best I pray for you.

Gentle David, never fear
To follow what is right and dear;
May you know content and bliss
With real happiness, as this.

May you always love and share,
Give little ones your utmost care
That you may live in this fair land;
Hills and burns you'll understand;
Geese to watch in evenings still;
Wrens and robins songs at Dusk
Where roses grow with monymusk.

Behold rich rainbows and the skies,
You'll know so much beyond them lies;
This land I pray ne'er harmed by wars
That leave their unrelenting scars.

Never forget, we've tried to give
Our best, that you may truly live.

December 1989

ALL THINGS VISIBLE AND INVISIBLE

August 1987

Sitting quietly in the Chancel of Dacre's ancient church once more with the door wide open, on an early morning, one is almost mesmerised gazing outside beyond the doorway with the timeless magic and tranquillity of a quiet country churchyard. Peace reigns as gentle breezes sing through meadow grasses and a host of wild flowers in a rhythm all of their own. Golden buttercups, dusky wine burnets, blue scabious reflecting patches of skies above, made more brilliant in their effect with drifting clouds creating patterns on the grass below. The hum of bees working among clover and among other scented flowers long established in God's acre. Words from the service remain for ever in my mind, "I believe in all things visible and invisible."

What words can be more true than these when working in a garden. Gardeners are a law unto themselves: they are always conscious of God's time, for seasons come and go with regularity: whatever may happen in the world beyond our hedgerows, we know that winter will surely follow the ripening of seeds and berries and the harvest of the land: winter's frost breaks down the good earth, causing plant life and all living things to rest or hibernate. But surely, with the first rays of sunshine, golden aconites are ready to leap into life, and we are unfailingly assured that spring is only just around the corner and life will return with renewed energy. The mysteries of the unseen; the return of swallows from far countries and so much more, over which man has no control; truly they bespeak the visible *and* the invisible.

We know full well that this is the time to take stock of our gardens for another year, to prune systematically amongst flowering shrubs such as thickets of philadelphus and many of the stronger species and shrub roses when flowering has passed. At this time of year foliage is more than ample, and we can recognise vigorous young wood searching for light, quite different in form and colour to old woody stems.

Where shrub and species roses have been planted in the last two or three years, they only require, on average, flowered branches cutting back to about three buds, but the more vigorous types in later years should have a certain amount of old hardened wood cut right back to where young wood has emerged, and the new wood shortened a little to make it branch. Of course there are so many species roses, each requiring to be treated individually: those of *moschata* varieties which are wreathed in garlands of glory for many weeks, scenting gardens with delicious fragrance, must be pruned severely for they grow at an alarming rate. Originating from China and the Far East, they are seen at their best wandering at will over a holly hedge or scrambling up and through old yew trees, their creamy white flower clusters often centred with yellow conspicuously beautiful against their dark green host. These "rough" roses must have old wood cut to the ground each autumn and young growth shortened back, while new growth emerging in the wrong direction may be tied in, or cut out also.

The more different old roses one plants, the more fascinating they become; most have histories, or names that recall some historical event. 'Mary Queen of Scots' evokes pictures of the beautiful young Queen whose life was short and sad but full of romance. Her rose may appear to the imaginative like a small single paeony, with a boss of pronounced stamens and prominent white eye surrounded by lilac petals each with reddish brushmarks. Later dark little fruits adorn this small plant whose origin and parentage is unknown.

Moss roses are fascinating also, 'Le Chapeau de Napoleon' being a useful, medium sized shrub; highly scented and once more a chance discovery in France in 1826; silvery, deep pink flowers enhanced with a mossy calyx which appears so like the pointed hat made famous by the Emperor. A wealth of roses of this date originated from French flowers, the soft double pink *'Amaieux'* being one of them — a short plant suitable for smaller gardens, a lovely shape, with purple-crimson striping, so appealing and eye-catching.

Useful ground is not lost beneath these dreams of beauty, for early spring flowers which later enjoy shady conditions can be grown close to the roots of taller shrub roses, besides groups of narcissi and miniature bulbs, bringing colour at all seasons. Blue-eyed brunneras and hostas of many varieties create splendid ground cover to keep weeds at bay. 'Thomas Hogg' is an attractive hosta; its broad cream-edged leaves and mauve flowers make a fine show, very useful for floral art. *Hosta undulata* (*H.* 'Mediovariegata') is more dwarf with prettily cream and green waved leaves, useful and decorative among small plants, or lending support while showing off the beauty of a single flower in a vase. Herbaceous geraniums also provide useful ground cover, providing delicious fragrance and colour. The musk *Geranium macrorrhizum* 'Ingwersen's Variety' has beautifully shaped aromatic foliage which colour richly with age, remaining brilliant till Christmas. Soft rose-pink flowers appear in early summer or late spring, becoming mounds of beauty and a very useful weed suppressor. This herbaceous geranium was produced by Mr Ingwersen, the well-known nurseryman who was extremely kind and helpful to me, when, as a child, I bought plants for my little garden from his stand in the Chelsea Show. Children never forget these occasions and little kindnesses.

G. 'Johnson's Blue', is still a favourite with its many ornamental deeply-divided leaves and cup-shaped flowers borne throughout summer. My newest beauty is *G. wallichianum* 'Buxton's Variety', whose blue saucer-like flowers with white centres trail over ground and among other plants for many weeks. Their flowers resemble nemophila, the much loved annual which children sow in their gardens. Stocks can be increased from internodal cuttings dibbled into a suitable frame; these are better undisturbed till the following autumn when strong root systems will have developed.

There are many hardy geraniums from which to choose. Many are beautiful when grown among shrub roses, some of which become resplendent with eye-catching hips and turning leaves matching the glory of geranium foliage and fragrance.

Such an assemblage of beauty will bring colour to our gardens over a long period.

OUR SECRET GARDEN

August 1988

While I was working in the garden re-staking delphiniums, members of a gardening club wandered leisurely among my flowers. Some of them stopped to talk. "This is such a lovely garden," one of them said, "it truly is a secret garden". "Do you remember the film *The Secret Garden*", chimed in another lady. "And do you remember that fascinating old book, *The Secret Garden*", I add, "we read it many times when we were children".

I began to realise more clearly that even to strangers, our garden really is, like a fascinating secret garden, though to me it often feels like this; there are so many turns and twists, hidden paths where one can walk comfortably amongst tall herbaceous plants, or even amongst thorny Scots briar roses. These visitors spoke of plants supporting each other, and nothing growing in straight lines. Plants were never meant to be regimented; many must act as "nurse" plants to protect more fragile neighbours. Most plants are settled in groups, giving a true display of their worth; only a few spectacular subjects are planted by themselves, but all used as ground cover in their own individual ways. It is pointless leaving unnecessary spaces for weeds when violets or members of the primula family could be used, besides giving these shade lovers the conditions they enjoy.

Someone asked if we grew carnations and what did we do with them after flowering. We only grow a few, from young shoots that appear on special bouquets that one of our family has been given. Some were from little Hermione's christening decorations, which is a lovely moment to perpetuate through plant life. This visitor told me that if one planted tired carnation plants directly into a border, in three weeks they would be blooming all over again, and mine certainly are enjoying their outdoor holiday.

Frequently, visitors are able to tell me most interesting pieces of information. The most fascinating occurrence was, as usual, by complete chance. I longed to know much more about some of our very ancient varieties of apple trees. Last September two people walked up the path where shrub roses grow in the former early vegetable border in front of wall-trained apple trees. They stopped to talk, asking me if I knew their names. A very old and most beautifully grown tree, I knew to be 'Peasgood Nonesuch'. "What a coincidence," this man exclaimed, "for I am Mr Peasgood, and my great-grandmother was *the* Mrs Peasgood who found this seedling apple. Her family were nursery-men living near Stamford. The apples this tree produced were of such perfect shape, so magnificent in size and quality that in France it was given the title 'Peasgood Nonpareil'; it was even exported to Russia for the Tzar's table." I could hardly believe my ears to be told all this by a *real* Mr Peasgood whose family had actually produced our tree. And to think that I might not have been in the garden at this very moment and missed the chance of talking with a most welcome visitor!

When I was a small child, I remember Will Stuart bringing these magnificent apples into the house for dinner parties, well polished before they left his care. I

Barton Fell from the park

Mecanopsis in the Knot Garden

Wild Garden from the Terrace

remember him talking about other varieties which he grew including 'Stirling Castle', 'Charles Ross' and others all bred soon after the turn of the nineteenth century. Ross became head gardener at Welford Park and bred many famous apples. He was born and brought up at Dalmeny on the Forth where his father managed the Earl of Rosebery's estate, and Stuart, also being trained in Scottish gardens, was probably encouraged by my Aunt Maud to plant trees that had been produced by his friends.

We still grow the delicious 'Keswick Codling', a warm yellow early cooker, which is quite the best variety to bake in a cool oven stuffed with sultanas and topped with golden syrup. 'Bramley Seedling' sees our apple crop through until Easter; the last of our original old Bramleys required to be felled last spring, but younger trees already bear bountiful crops; the original of the species resulted from a chance sowing of a pip into a pot somewhere between 1809 and 1813 by Betsy Brailford who had a cottage garden in Church Street, Southwell, Nottinghamshire. The well-known fruit grower, Merryweather, introduced this great apple, which would be sadly missed almost two hundred years later. Mother expected our apple crop to see us through each winter, and Bramleys filled the bill.

It is important that apple houses are fumigated and shelves thoroughly scrubbed with Jeyes Fluid in good time, before one can thankfully sing "All is safely gathered in".

APPLE HARVEST

How wise Victorian gardeners were
    In knowledge and in working ways,
Selecting various apple trees
    To fill their well-scrubbed, slatted trays.
Large households would expect there'd be
Apples to use, each month, you'll see.

Good gard'ners friends lived far and wide
    Exchanging plants and cuttings too:
Some nurserymen made annual calls
    Each garden's need, they really knew:
Where frost struck late and winter long,
Trees needed constitutions strong.

Those early apples on the wall,
    Delight of all who passed nearby,
High summer with her artist's brush
    Touched them with rubied dawn-drawn sky.
While 'Keswick Codlings', buttered green
Gave cook a meal to suit a Queen.

Proud 'Peasgood' ripened on the wall,
    Her apple filled a gold-rimmed plate,
Were gathered gently, lest they fall,
    These flame, gold beauties, never late,
Such previous jewels of Tsarist pride,
Sweet 'Non Pareil' in France, beside.

'Duchess of Kent', her russet fame
    Eats like a treat at Christmas time;
'Deux Ans' from Ireland's Emerald Isle,
    'Rival' and 'Grieve' and more to ryhme:
The keeping 'Stirling Castle's' tray
Was gathered at a later day.

At Harvest Festival in church
    Apples like jewels, among fresh flowers,
Perfect and polished, proffered in joy
    Work of much pride and countless hours.
Men gathered fruit on different days,
Each tree must grow in their own sweet ways.

Hard 'Bramley Seedlings' loosed their stems
　　To feed the house till Easter fell.
Old Warner's King' and 'Bismarck' too
　　Ready to store e're frost befell.
Then Dalemain rang with Harvest cup
For all was safely gathered up.

Pruning took long, with special knives,
　　Some branches spurred when sap flowed down;
Tar oil and spray while days were still
　　Farm yard manure when leaves turned brown.
Apple House full, rejoiced to tell
Of fragrance rich, now all was well.

May 6th 1991

CREATIVE JOYS IN THE GARDEN

August 1986

This is the time of year to take cuttings of all sorts of plants and shrubs, both hardy and semi-hardy. One has so many treasures in the garden that one is somewhat doubtful of some of them surviving long, cold winters, particularly much loved herbs such as rosemary — a little batch of these lined out in a cold frame, or dibbled round the edge of a pot and overwintered in a cold greenhouse, may just provide a much wanted collection of nice young plants to put out in mid June, — not before, — which will make one feel thankful of having made the effort, especially when one's old favourite bush has lost all its will to live.

Propagating is the most fascinating and satisfying art of gardening. We are all economical by nature, and to be able to give a friend something which one values and which one has managed, artfully, to produce oneself, gives untold pleasure. I find that cuttings can be taken at all sorts of odd moments, not just at the official time of early autumn. This is much easier, because one can take bits of this and that when time allows. It is important to take cuttings when plant life still retains the urge to grow and produce rootlets whereby it can survive winter conditions, instead of sadly browning off and losing the will to live.

One does not need fancy artifices to propagate. A small area of nicely cultivated soil with a fair amount of peat or leaf mould and plenty of sharp sand, so that the soil has that lovely, friable, feeling when trickling through one's fingers. These beds should get plenty of light, but be preferably situated against a shady wall; alternatively if this is not possible, one can shade it with fine-mesh plastic netting about three feet above the bed so that fresh air circulates. The soil must be nicely firmed, but not unattractively tight and hard, for remember you are dealing with very young things, learning to stand on their own feet.

Into this medium all sorts of hardwood cuttings can be dibbled; the cut surfaces, below a node dipped lightly into rooting powder which speeds up the dangerous period of "waiting."

Cuttings will probably only require to be four or five inches long, the bottom two-thirds of the cutting having its leaves cleanly removed. Never allow cuttings to dry out; take a little bucket of water around with you as you gather pieces of this and that. At this time of year, many shrubs are still making young extension growth. In preparing your cuttings, they should be shortened from the tip, back to a pair of leaves composed of the tougher mature quality you are looking for.

One of my favourite shrub roses, the species *Rosa farrerii*, is very temperamental to root. This Chinese rose is one of the most beautiful of all shrub roses, with quantities of fern-like foliage, which turn wonderful colours as autumn approaches. Quantities of tiny, pink flowers give it the fascinating name the the Threepenny Bit Rose. Originally cuttings were taken in autumn from my initial plant, and frequently these never grew; then I started to experiment with material which was nice and firm but was covered with energetic spring growth. The urge to survive is strong, and these "took" magnificently. I wanted to make a hedge of this rose to shelter a circle of beds surrounding our great well-head at Huntfield. Wind is our chief adversary and hedges within hedges are ideal. So, one May time, I dipped suitable cuttings into rooting powder and "stuck" them in with sharp sand where they were to grow. The result is fairylike; these lovely branches forming a tough hedge which is clipped gently to keep it within bounds. Otherwise, *Rosa farreii* grows into a huge bush whose latent leaves sparkle with sunlit snow, or magical pearly drops of rain, even in winter time.

A cold frame is the other most useful place for rooting somewhat more tender cuttings. This can be blanketed during the worst of winter and preferably should not face the south in the way in which so many old fashioned frames were built. Cuttings must not dry out, but once they are "in" and watered, that should suffice for a long period. Circulation of air is very important at all seasons to prevent those unwanted moulds to take over and destroy all one's work.

Subjects like lavender respond well to the protection of a cold frame in a more sunlit situation since they are sunlovers. From mid August to early September gives the highest "take", and it makes all the difference if the stock plants are young; two year old plants are ideal, and it will do the parents more good than harm to remove numerous young shoots. Santolina, the silver cotton lavender, clematis, ballota, daphnes, — the possibilities are legion. When cuttings are dibbled closely in rows, they respond far better than being potted in isolation. It is as if they, like children, enjoy each other's company.

One word of warning. Do not expect your cuttings to be ready to move or pot on when spring comes. Those that have survived and are showing obvious signs of growth must be left till June or even later when they have had time to "stand on their own feet". Sometimes one must wait even longer to be really sure and not waste all one's labours.

It is all so exciting to attempt what in earlier days may have seemed impossible, but one never stops learning, — and also learning from making mistakes.

LITTLE ONES

Dear robin with your cheerful face
You're ever in my every place;
Wher'ere I dig, or fork and hoe
You dig for worms, and on we go.

My barrowful of weeds is rich
With worms to toss and seeds to stitch
When greenhouse door stands open wide
There's always bugs and feasts inside.

That shallow pool outside the door
Is where you bathe and ask for more;
You wash and splash and preen your wing
Before 'tis time to sit and sing.

The sweetest song composed for me
Before we make for house and tea.
"You won't forget my breakfast too
That I may sing and work with you."

When all the children go to bed
You whistle on the wall instead,
And after games and little prayers
They slowly climb the topmost stairs
While tucked up tight, and stories sing,
You warm your head beneath your wing.

1987

PLANTS FOR FREE

September 1988

This is an excellent time of year to take cuttings from favourite plants, perhaps because of doubtful hardiness; if these are dibbled into a cold frame, or into pots or boxes in the greenhouse, they will ensure a good supply to bring colour to your garden in the future. Or perhaps one needs to increase stock of some precious acquisition. Everything is worth trying and if one only has fifty percent success one gets so much pleasure from being able to "do it yourself."

Cuttings may be taken at various times during the growing season and frequently I dibble in a few during May and June with great success, for at that season everything is growing abundantly. There is no need to stick to the book, but some cuttings are more certain of success taken from ripened shoots on stems that have finished flowering, when the entire energy of the plant is going to produce ripened growth which will withstand wintery conditions, or else into its seedpods. Cuttings vary from 1 to 4 inches in length and are usually pulled from the parent stem with a heel. Lower leaves are removed and the heel or cut dipped in rooting powder. I keep a frame with plenty of sharp sand incorporated with the soil, in which to pop cuttings at any time. For those expected to root during the summer the frame must be out of direct sunlight.

One must not expect woody cuttings, such as lavender, to be ready to plant out in May; mine were only properly rooted by August, and these will be useful plants next spring: but softer items, such as pansies and penstemons are usually ready to move on by early June.

Really woody cuttings, such as shrub roses, will take two to three years before one can move them safely, but these are best rooted in a sandy corner of the garden where snow can blanket and protect. Snow has wonderful properties for cleansing and invigorating. Buddleias are easily propagated from cuttings. The spectacular glowing purple-red *B. davidii* 'Nanho Purple' growing at Dalemain, gave me a really good offspring to take to my Scottish garden.

The most amazing piece of luck was a large piece of my yellow tree paeony, *P. lutea Ludlowii*, which broke off just before I was about to pack up and once again leave for Huntfield. I hadn't much time so put it into the car and planted it reasonably deeply in its new environment. These large and very beautiful shrubs, with deeply lobed ornamental leaves, usually have buds at the base of their woody stems. The following spring the branch began to grow and has become a handsome shrub. Since that amazing shot in the dark, several other pieces have been rooted where they will have plenty of room to develop without taking over much more than their allotted space among shrub roses, or else they are planted in my woodland Grove. *P. lutea ludlowii* is grown just as much for its large leaves which are deeply divided into pointed leaflets as for its bowl-shaped flowers which glow in sunlight. Within two or three years these broken-off pieces will have become magnificent shrubs.

This is also the time of year to prune rambler roses, cutting out old flowering wood to the base as in the case of those of *R. wichuriana*, while those whose new growth occurs higher should only be cut to a strong dormant bud. Some of my shrub roses produced tremendously long, new growth this wet summer which have been cut back considerably to encourage the remaining growth to form good side shoots on which they should flower abundantly. Pruning varies from rose to rose, but it is much pleasanter to give them individual treatment in warm weather.

The wonderful *R. moschata 'Floribunda'* whose stems are wreathed in clusters of almost primrose-like flowers, is treated like wichuriana ramblers, some of the old growth being cut to the ground. This rampant rose looks wonderful on a high wall, or trailing downwards over a low wall; it is ideal to grow against the dark back-cloth of yew trees.

A very fine double form of our native king cup *Caltha palustris* 'Flore Pleno' has seeded plentifully in a damp gravel path. This magnificent form grows in a damp border beside our sun parlour which we use so much for meals; special plants in this alpine border and nearby wild garden give us the most pleasure, being alongside the house. This long lasting plant forms splashes of brilliant orange-yellow so when time allows, seedlings must be carefully lined out for future use.

FOR SAYA

aged nine

A little girl with dancing gait,
Sweet Saya sings with merry smile;
Her lilting laugh and winning ways
Those tales she tells with sweet beguile.

'Round fields and woods she loves to ride;
On windswept fields her ponies roam
With David, racing, "Who can win,"
They ride the heathered hills of home.

Their baby brother held most dear
She'll dress and feed and rock to sleep;
Or carry round with tenderness
'Ere shining stars begin to peep.

Her long fair hair as sunlight gleams
Like rose buds, in the month of May;
All draped around her fragile frame
She fills each moment of the day.

In harmony with small brown wrens,
Those little songs I hear her sing,
Unlocks within my heart a chord
Like sunbeams in awak'ning spring.

May you protected always be
In life's unseen, uncertain ways;
And ever come back safely home
To fill our lives with gladsome days.
But now, when you are young and small
May nothing tear your life apart
Through storms and sunlight all your days
I'll hold you closely to my heart.

November 26th 1989

A FEW OF THOSE OTHER
MECONOPSIS SPECIES

August 1990

Although one frequently thinks of Himalayan poppies only, as being those glorious blue herbaceous plants to be seen growing in damp woodland surroundings where there is plenty of humus, or in well-mulched borders, there are many differing species also.

Some are extremely difficult to grow, others requiring scree conditions. *Meconopsis bella* is one of these, a desirable dwarf species bearing pink or blue flowers; its habitat is shaded rock crevices where an exceptionally long tap root is slowly produced before establishing itself securely. *M. dhwojii* is monocarpic, one of the type of plants which take two or three years to reach flowering, only to die after ripening and scattering seed: its graceful panicles of cup-shaped flowers are pale yellow. *M. horridula*, a monocarpic deciduous species, is to be found in variable shades of blue, from silver to deepest royal blue. My old friend, Sir George Taylor, one time Director of the Royal Horticultural Society, worked on this genus with devotion, eventually joining an expedition to Bhutan where he found a yellow form of the widespread *M. horridula*. This species is most satisfactory when grown in scree conditions in full sun, but give of their best in good rich soil. Some are found on elegant flowering spikes, or it can be a coarse, heavy plant; its straplike, dissected leaves are covered in coarse spines, their colours varying according to their locality from yellow, pure pink, or chocolate, to a light blue in high altitudes.

Monocarpic species are frequently woolly haired, rosette forming: they are better protected from heavy rain in winter, with a cloche. In natural conditions they sow seed freely and survive. *M. integrifolia*, George Farrer's Lampshade Poppy, is a beautiful, yellow monocarpic species. Oval, hairy leaves can be delicate pastel shades of pink, blues or gold when emerging in spring, expanding into rosettes of leaves, covered with pale yellow hairs. Flower buds and young leaves are vulnerable to frost, and should frost fall at the wrong moment, flowers will develop in a distorted manner and die without setting seed. Usually, glorious flower stems arise from basal scapes, though most flowers elongate from a central stem. It is relatively easy to grow from seed.

M. regia is an evergreen species. Its large yellow flowers are sometimes red, growing from an evergreen rosette which can reach four feet. Covered by thick golden hairs which glow in frosty weather, it takes between three to five years before the flowering stem emerges.

These are but a few of the wonderful meconopsis family, endemic to parts of the Himalayas, particularly the mountainous part of China, abutting on to Tibet, as well as those of Burma and Assam. The arid Tibetan plateau is also, strangely, the home of a few species, only one as yet being endemic. So much is yet to be discovered in this amazing region of tropical, mountain forests: who knows what other plants are growing happily in such secret surroundings?

GARDENING WITH RABBITS

August 1990

Rabbits! Those fascinating cosy-coated little creatures, who sit up on our lawns and wash their faces, are a terrible pest in so many gardens; it is frequently impossible to keep them out effectively. Our drive traverses through woodlands opening on to lawns and borders around the house. What can we grow in these borders which will not provide a tasty meal?

Over the years I have tried to grow "non-edible" rabbit food outside the protection of the walled garden with great success. The most exotically beautiful of these plants are Himalayan blue poppies, *Meconopsis baileyii*, George Sheriff's *M. grandis* or Cicely Crewdson's blue, which reflect early summer skies: in fact, any member of this marvellous family. They easily form large clumps in cool, reasonably moist soil, of which the soil in our "semi-wild garden" is composed, where beds and borders have formulated and grown adjacent to lawns and rough grass at Huntfield. Yellow Welsh poppies seed themselves in gravel paths, where packet sown Shirley poppies also grow happily.

One large bed of meconopsis is bordered by *Sedum* 'Autumn Joy', astilbes, and with polyanthus to provide colour over many months.

Paeonies are one of my joys. These now fill a narrow border which is backed by a low, flag-topped wall; there very old jardinieres sit, filled with double pink geraniums and the useful trailing variegated nepeta. Herbaceous geraniums are ever useful. That great plantsman, Mr Ingwersen, gave so many gems to the gardening world. His musk geranium, *G. macrorrhizum*, with lilac pink flowers, is especially useful to the wild gardener. I have a very "difficult" border, and this lovely, leaf-scented plant layers its rhizomes at ground level providing a weed smothering edging, behind which thornier stemmed shrub roses grow which rabbits do not relish. It is useless to plant roses which produce succulent young growth at ground level: there are dozens of moss and species roses whose stems are thorny, from which to choose a wide selection. Some modern shrub roses also answer the call, such as the magnificent 'Cerise Bouquet', whose twelve feet, arching branches, wreathed in scented blooms, will deter everything, even deer, with her jagged thorns. If one feels at all anxious when planting newcomers, it is easy enough to encircle them with netting until safely established.

Netting must be used where lilies are planted, for it is not only rabbits which nip the young shoots, but roe deer which pass by in early summer dawnings, biting off flowers of only certain varieties. My beautiful regal blossoms and others are left lying where they fell. So each group of lilies must have wire for complete protection. This becomes quickly disguised by a wealth of azaleas, primulas, hardy pale pink fuchsias, astilbes and tall campanulas.

What of hardy agapanthus, the Blue Lily of the Nile? I have plenty to spare for my trial and error experiments: they have since formed good clumps and rabbits pass them by. Likewise, those colourful bedding begonias. I remember these plants growing in round beds on an unfenced lawn where my grandparents lived at

Lanrick, in Perthshire, beside the great river Teith. The word Lanrick means "a clearing in the forest", for the original fortress, around which the later castle was built, was the stronghold of the MacGregor clan, their graveyard encircled by ancient yew trees still in evidence not far from the Castle. Trees and plants grow magnificently in rich acid soil, where we grandchildren stayed so often.

So, emulating these beds on the lawns at Lanrick, I planted a group of begonias in early June, oblivious to rabbits: as all went well a further planting round the edge of a wide curved border where blue poppies had earlier bloomed, was successfully kirtled with a quantity of these useful, colourful plants.

Willow gentians, those herbaceous gems whose two foot stems of blue are a picture from August onwards, together with a cluster of fragrant double pink meadowsweet; nearby a trial plant of an ornamental, variegated figwort, whose cream and green leaves bring light to a dull corner; Philadelphus, deutzias, berberis, variegated dogwoods, golden and other ornamental elders grow untouched, providing shelter for smaller plants. Golden St John's Wort, 'Hidcote' variety, makes a great show, three feet high and wide, while the old pink *Rosa officinalis* has room to spread her suckering shoots. Hostas in great variety act as weed smotherers.

Our house walls are festooned with plants: tropaeoleum spreading her "dustsheet" of flame flowers throughout an old herring-boned cotoneaster which plays the long-suffering host; *Clematis* x *jackmanii* likewise scrambles. Most clematis are carefully sited and given tree guards to protect the first two feet of growth.

Possibilities are legion, so never say "My garden is impossible!" — as long as the New Dawn rose showers her blossoms around our windows I will be a happy gardener.

CARNIVAL

My garden is aflame with latent flowers;
October's warmth brings Harvest Festival
Where bees hum still, these shortened daylight hours
Their merry song of timeless carnival.

From flower to flower along the borders go
With rhythmic joy, as like an organ floats
'cross shadowed garden in the sunlit glow,
Their honeyed song of softly dreaming notes.

Loud trumpets, deep blue gentians wake and call,
And clarinets of lilies join their theme;
Red roses in the gall'ry, on the wall;
Delphiniums, tall, a late and added dream;
Round ripened riches, feasts of berries; butterflies
Of brilliant shades and outstretched fragile wings
All seeing with a thousand eyes
Like ladybirds, and countless moving things.

Knee deep in stands of russet, scented grass
Hang spiders webs, translucent, wondrous fair,
Sway gently with each little winds that pass,
Like needlework of ceaseless toil and care.

Then, through old trees gold, dazzling sunlight streams,
Wide stretching in the ever changing light,
Cast shadows on the lawn, as precious dreams,
Wish closing petalled flowers, a safe goodnight.

October 1990

SEASON OF MELLOW FRUITFULNESS

September 1986

Autumn is truly the season of mellow fruitfulness when hard-working gardeners feel justified in sitting in a comfortable seat amongst deliciously fragrant flowers in order to contemplate handiwork of the past year, wondering where we have room to plant yet another tree or shrub admired in a friend's garden, or to imitate something exotically beautiful, once seen and never forgotten. This is the time of year to plan ahead, and any additions must be thought of as architectural features, adding further bone structure, or among little gems to bring brilliance of colour into unattractive corners.

As we sit and dream, our thoughts wander like butterflies flitting from momentary floral perches. The countryside is so mature, even if somewhat overgrown; there is a feeling of complete satisfaction especially in the world of nature beyond the perimeter of the garden. Plants and trees have given of their best: it is the season of harvest festival along hedgerows; bees are busily amassing pollen to manufacture honey, creating perfect drowsy harmony. Centuries past, Virgil, philosopher and thinker, while writing and considering their amazing industry, exclaimed, "O truly blessed and marvellous mother-bee!" and so she is; and all her tribe. How sad that so many hives died in the bitter cold of last winter, and what a loss are their untimely deaths throughout our countryside.

What extra colour and flamboyance can we bring to harvest festivals in our own plots? The versatile family of maples are truly ornamental. An extensive genus, mostly hardy and of easy culture, but some of the Japanese *Acer palmatum* species require shelter especially during their first winters, until firmly established on their own roots. Our garden at Huntfield, being a thousand feet above sea level and on the north side of the hills, provides wonderful, easily worked, dark acid soil, ideal for so many plants, but here, winter is a testing time.

A.p. 'Dissectum Atropurpureum' is a glorious shrub, well worth all the efforts of building a wigwam of light posts surrounded by fir branches to encompass its frail form. This was constructed faithfully for seven winters until our eye-catching maple grew too tall, forming a high dense crown of glowing leaves and branches, growing firmly on its own roots.

A.p. 'Senkaki', the glorious irridescent Coral-Barked Maple, has survived three long cold, winters at Dalemain, its wigwam remaining surely in place until all frosts are past; a neighbouring juniper, *Juniperus* x *media* 'Gold Sovereign', with low spreading foliage, gives added warmth.

On the other hand, many picturesque, medium sized maples, such as *A. campestre*, the Field or Hedge Maple, are completely hardy, the foliage of this species turning clear yellow, flushed with red at this season.

Beautifully coloured suckers on the roots of standard Acer campestre, which would, in nature, form a thicket, should be removed. If grown on in a cutting bed for a year they form strong plants to be used as trees or for hedging elsewhere.

Magnolias have been treated with the same respect, as are the less hardy Far Eastern maples, in our gardens, choosing not only sheltered sites but species whose flowers, in all probability, miss late frosts. *Magnolia wilsonii*, a large wide-spreading shrub introduced from Western China in 1908, is dream-like in early June; pendulous, saucer-shaped flowers are white with a boss of crimson stamens creating a marvellous effect for many weeks.

Rowans are making colourful displays along motorways and throughout the countryside. Why not consider planting one of horticultural merit of which nowadays there are many, frequently grown for their ornamental foliage and loose drooping clusters of differently coloured fruits. *Sorbus vilmorinii* is a beautiful small tree of elegant habit becoming a certain feature in any garden. Its fernlike foliage becomes red and purple, while panicles of rose-red fruits gradually change from pink in colour, to white, flushed with rose; a charming species for the smaller garden introduced in 1889 from Western China, where so many treasures have been discovered.

It was the Abbé Delavay, a hard working missionary, who found this Sorbus amid many other new plants. He was not a botanist, but his hobby was collecting plants and seeds which eventually found their way back to Paris. In due course they came into the capable hands of the distinguished botanist, Monsieur A. Frandhet in the late nineteenth century, and because of his industry, these exotics became available to gardeners all over the world.

There are so many smaller plants other than trees which bring joy and colour in the autumn. That low growing creeping spurge *Euphorbia cyparissias*, turns the colour of ripe corn. Last winter was unkind to this "furry" friend which provides ground cover for so many endearing spring bulbs. It seemed to have very nearly given up the will to live, but being of a patient nature, I am always prepared to wait and hope that early summer sunshine will encourage a resurrection. Somewhat later than usual, those endearing furry shoots and flat-faced yellow flowers tinged with coral, were carpeting their allotted space.

Lilies have been particularly good these last weeks; they are not as difficult to grow as many people think. *Lilium candidum*, the white chalice-like Madonna lily, so fragrant to the passer-by, has caused many to stand and wonder at its beauty. They have given no trouble, planted in a shady bed beside a young *Magnolia sieboldii*, each bulb buried with a generous amount of sharp sand to give drainage and to prevent bulbs from rotting in continuous wet weather. Yellow L. 'Golden Clarion,' with trumpet-shaped flowers, have grown successfully for several years, sheltered and protected by low growing mounds of Scots briar roses which sucker freely, providing added drainage. 'Limelight', too, with pendulous trumpet-shaped flowers, creates an exclusive picture, while 'Enchantment' not only produces many upturned nasturtium-flame flowers on every stem, but has grown into a solid clump of bulbs. Once more, nurse plants are provided by azaleas, while, at a little distance, silver variegated dogwood *Cornus elegantissima*, acts as a hedge-like windbreak so necessary in our climate.

Perhaps during this season of autumn, which the poet John Keats describes as "close bosomed friend of the maturing sun", a few of these plants, which have been already "well tried out", will find their way into other readers' gardens.

BOUNTIFUL HARVEST OF OUR GARDENS

September 1990

Last roses of summer are still blooming to perfection, their fragrance more precious than those we gathered many weeks ago. *R.* 'Alberic Barbier' rambling against a low wall, and another clothing an archway with superb glossy foliage, are to me the most perfect, for their creamy white flowers, flushed lemon yellow, bloom long into autumn when other roses are past. Bred by M. Barbier in France around 1900, its seed parent *R. wichuraiana* came from the Far East, the origin of so many "old" roses. This sunkissed rose is thus related to old favourites including 'Albertine', 'Emily Gray' and 'New Dawn'. It will grow up a north wall and is well worth a place of honour in our gardens.

Nearby, I was weeding a narrow, sunny border with a little wall behind where the low growing, rambling *Geranium Wallichianum* 'Buxtons Variety' grows to perfection. Sky blue, buttercup-like flowers with white centres repose and shine in evening sunlight, for the plant produces runners, like strawberries, which enjoy spreading themselves across the soft, blue-green, fern-like foliage of *Euphorbia cyparissias*, whose yellow flowers are a past memory. This comfortable, low growing perennial, growing along the top of the little wall, is very happy to display these enchanting nemophila-like flowers. Their flowered "runners" can be cut off and rooted in a cold frame.

These present weeks are a good time to take cuttings of numerous plants. I dug a barrowload of rotted leafmould mixed with some good soil and sharp sand — nice and gritty — into a couple of frames, making them quite firm in readiness for cuttings. Dip their tips into rooting powder before dibbling them in firmly, where most should remain till early summer before they become properly rooted and safe to leave their nursery bed.

My favourite, *G.W.* 'Buxton's Variety', went into the frame first, any remaining flower buds being snipped off with scissors. Dr Walich who discovered this plant was a director of the Botanical Gardens in Calcutta.

Penstemons, a great favourite for bedding out when I was a child, are once again in the forefront. Most are hardy perennials, overwintering successfully with a good mulch; but in our northern parts of Britain it is wise to take cuttings of the larger flowered varieties. Many cuttings are now suitably long enough to pull off flowered stems, with a "heel" which makes for easy rooting.

We have grown the elegant, slender stemmed *P.* 'Garnet' for many years. Cuttings of these soon make lovely bushy plants, amongst which tulips can be grown most successfully. The newer *P.* 'Snowstorm' has provided a lot of cuttings even though I have only a few plants. Its flurry of clear white trumpets are in evidence in the Knot Garden, enclosed by sweet smelling box hedging, interplanted with silvery, filigree foliage of *Artemesia schmidtiana* 'Nana' which form little mounds. Once again tulips or smaller bulbs can be interplanted and remain in the ground to multiply. Some of the smaller alliums, particularly the cornflower blue *A. azureum*, make useful summer additions. Alliums belong to the onion family, and are to be found in many

Old China Blush rose, planted c. 1880

In the Walled Garden, Huntfield

Rosa 'Anna Louisa'

shapes, sizes and colours. I am frequently asked by visitors to the garden, "Could you tell me what those are?" The taller silvery lilac *A. albopilosum* is much admired. They are mostly found in bulb catalogues, although many gardeners are not aware of their existence.

Achilleas are another useful border plant which can easily be grown from cuttings. These are once more pulled off flower stems with a heel, or even cut from the tips of the wealth of younger growth at this time of year. The older golden variety is still as useful as later varieties such as clear light yellow *A*. 'Moonshine', flowering early, even in a hot sunny border like the one on the Terrace at Dalemain. They can be cut back to produce more flowers and silvery filigree foliage. Their cut flowers are useful when dried for winter decoration and look good amongst dark, shining leaved sprays of holly. The Greek hero, Achilles, was said to be the first to use these plants in medicine.

One of autumn's glories is the Scottish flame-flower, known frequently as tropaeoleum, to which family it belongs. Its glorious profusion of blooms scramble over any suitable host plant. They look lovely clinging on to a yew hedge, but the trouble is that the yew must be cut early in the summer so that this soft stemmed climber's extensive growth is not damaged. It enjoys a cool root run like clematis. My original plant was given to me by an old lady from her apple orchard where it grew profusely; she told me that it must be moved in its own soil, then planted in its new home. Mine was easily established among old rhododendrons on the edge of gravel at Huntfield. From there it spreads its wealth like a dust sheet dropping hard coated blue-black seeds in winter. These can only be moved when well sprouted, possibly in April. Seedlings were easily moved to another cool gravelly situation among herringbone cotoneasters and late flowering purple clematis on the house wall, facing west.

THE TEACHER

Drink deep, these mystic moods of autumn,
Long shadows, clear and deep across the hills.
Dark Corries, hid, as if behind
Veiled curtains of immortal life, that thrills
Wide heathered heights: their festal stage
Calls, witness be each peerless page

Drink deeper still with thankful hearts
Fulfilment of the seasons year;
Resurgent from long winter's rest
When spring's sown seeds will rise to bear
Rich fruits, ripe grains, their harvest yields
From woods and hills and golden fields.

Weep not, nor mourn the passing year,
Nor life's short hours to play our parts:
Is not the glory of each autumn there
To turn all sadness from our hearts:
Each ripening bud, each freshly gathered corn
Assures our resurrection, too, is born.

November 1989

NEW JOYS FOR OLD GARDENS

October 1990

Autumn's loveliness has been greatly enhanced by lack of frost. Berries in rich coats are conspicuous while herbaceous plants retire to bed, casting off the glamour of summertime, thus encouraging gardeners to plant more of these easy-to-care-for shrubs. Cotoneasters are a large family of decorative shrubs. *C. frigidus* is one of the most handsome; a tall semi-evergreen species with white flowers freely produced in May followed by quite large hanging clusters of scarlet berries. *C. x.* 'cornubia' is another one to be admired, especially when laden with berries, I planted it years ago as a half standard in a border amongst roses and phloxes, but with necessary pruning, its arching branches have formed themselves into the shape of a cave. Being semi-evergreen, this "cave" will make an excellent winter shelter for pots of lilies which require to be covered with leafmould in order to keep frost and wind at bay, and yet allowing the benefits of air and water which they need; meanwhile those precious lily bulbs are resting and multiplying in their restrictive homes. Frequently my pots of lilies and hydrangeas are also stored in the hollow of huge old holly bushes where they have never taken any harm and are in much better condition than if wintered in a greenhouse.

Cotoneasters and many other shrubs can be increased by cuttings of ripe growth in autumn, dibbled into a cold frame or into a sheltered place out of doors. They will take two growing seasons to make good plants.

Ornamental elder cuttings are rooted in the same way. Variegated gold- or silver-leaved hybrids make beautiful foliage plants, creating a brilliant effect for a very long season; in addition, their clusters of rich yellow or cream flowers play their part in April and May. They may be grown in tubs with great effect and pruned as desired. I am becoming more drastic with pruning many shrubs and climbing plants. When we first came to live at Huntfield thirty-two years ago, I considered it was so kind of my many plants and shrubs to grow so magnificently at a thousand feet above sea level, and, on the north side of the hills, and was somewhat loath to prune perhaps as much as I might have done. In most gardens shelter is needed above all things, and this one can provide by choosing from the enormous variety of shrubs available when so many of us are gardening mad. If one roots cuttings one can afford to throw something away that is unsuitable for its allotted space.

More slender plants have benefited from the long summer. My new Bleeding Hearts, *Dicentra macrocarpus* 'Himalayan Wonder' is scrambling over a dwarf, or now not so dwarf, golden juniper. Being also yellow-flowered, it looks very effective, growing somewhat like the elegant *Clematis macropetala*. This native of Nepal, growing in open situations at elevations from 1,350m to 2,850m is new to cultivation in Britain, and it may need some winter protection; at Dalemain it is scrambling through a low growing *Cotoneaster dammeri* whose dark, green, evergreen leaves, covered with rich ruby berries, will provide good winter shelter.

It is always fun to try something new, and last January Mr Robert Bolton, the sweet pea specialist from Birdbrook in Essex, wrote to tell me that he has two new sweet peas for 1991 and would like to name one 'Dalemain' and one 'Sylvia Mary', if we would agree. We were so overjoyed at such an honour to be bestowed on our garden and our home, I collapsed on Bryce's ever-welcome shoulder, into tears of pleasure. So, when in due course the catalogue came off the printer's line, we were sent an early copy; the outside cover portrayed our very own sweet peas in full colour: inside, with descriptions, a drawing of Dalemain as seen from the coach road bridge across Dacre Beck. This sweet pea is a rich ruby colour and the flowered sprays are a marvel of size and floriferousness. Rich rose cerise with rose pink at the base of the wings are the colours of my own sweet pea, which abound in glorious profusion.

   We only hope that we can grow these sweet peas to as high a degree of perfection as possible, for I am sure that Mr and Mrs Bolton will come north to visit us, when we hope we can show them bowls of these fragrant beauties gracing the house and giving so much pleasure to our many visitors. When he comes north, Mr Bolton will be visiting his old childhood haunts, for his great-grandmother's family were called Lynn and they were drapers in the main street of Penrith. His paternal family originated near Clitheroe in Lancashire, but moved south to a drier climate more suitable for growing sweet peas commercially.

FOR A LOVE OF TWO LANDS

As we drove over the Beef Tub
The sun and the heavens shone clear
While the devil was sleeping right soundly
On this feast of St Crispin, I hear.

The peace of October's late sunshine
Reflected and danced on the hills
Where rich bountiful harvests of autumn
Her purpose of seedtime fulfils.

These glorious lands of the Borders
Where our spirits will ceaselessly roam —
But as we came over the summit
I could see those dear hills of my home.

Blencathra and Carrock and Scawfell,
I gazed on my birthlands anew,
When Beyond these, lay Martindale's Forest —
They were urgently beckoning too.

My love is as deep as the waters
That flow in a fresh lakeland stream,
And as deep as a clear Border river
In a life that must pass as a dream.

My love is held fast in the Borders,
While my heart is held fast in the lakes
But whenever each canvas lies opened
My wandering spirit awakes.

See the sunlight and cloudlight aroving,
Kiss those green hills, and blue hills with sun,
While the wild geese fly high, 'cross both sea and the sky
Fuse our deep rooted loves into one.

AUTUMN'S JOYOUS FESTIVAL

September 1986

Autumn's bounteous beauty, so rich in ever-changing colours, warm and usually calm, almost emotional is her intensity, so often an artist's dream of perfection. The tremendous feeling of fulfilment is almost comparable with the joy of a mother and her precious new-born babe — the satisfaction that so much has been accomplished.

It is an exciting season too, for all around us in the countryside fields of corn are newly harvested, but in many cases stubbles are hastily ploughed out, so that next season's crop can be sown, allowing seeds to germinate rapidly, reaping the reward of beneficial sunshine before frost and snow become the order of the day. However inconvenient, frost and snow are essential to re-invigorate well-worn, and perhaps over-cultivated soil.

In our gardens glowing colours bring a sense of thanks-giving and pleasure; not only the richness of late summer flowers, but the brilliance of leaves also, some appearing as if they are on fire as sunlight streams through their ever-changing forms. Nights turn cold as the harvest moon almost turns the small hours of night into daylight with awesome brilliance. Late crops of runner beans will be frosted and dahlias blackened, but we must not lament — we must look ahead with faith in the promise of another spring. With knowledge acquired over many years, we can understand how to care for the good earth without spoiling its natural potentials.

Every living creature must have rest at some period in its existence — plant life is no exception. Winter provides this enforced rest, as autumn slows down their mechanism. When this period of drowsiness is fulfilled, one can prune unwanted branches without the risk of "bleeding"; at an earlier season, to undertake such harsh treatment causes sap, the life blood of trees, to seep out, and rot the very tree we are attempting to make more beautiful — to our way of thinking.

Pruning is a very necessary, comfortably warm, task to accomplish when one cannot do much else in the garden. One plants small shrubs, and a few years later they have outgrown their allotted space. One must prune the lower branches of trees and shrubs to desired shapes. Ornamental miniature conifers are some of the worst offenders, however beautiful they are. Many years ago my sister planted the beautiful Colorado Blue Spruce, *Picea pungens*, at Dalemain, where alpine flowers were intended to grow. Now this conifer is at least twenty feet high and has not only had its lower branches removed, but its greedy roots have made it impossible to grow anything close by. These supposedly dwarf conifers are extremely ornamental, lending architectural feature in a garden, but one must plant warily, or be prepared to remove offending over-growing "miniature conifers."

Another ornamental blue spruce was added to our collection recently, *Picea onicum*, but this "miniature" was planted in grass where it may grow unhindered in future years.

One must prune with care and and plant with foresight. Kolkwitzia (Caprifoliacea), the Beauty Bush, is one of the loveliest shrubs, in a genus of one species. Covered with pale pink bell-shaped flowers in early summer, its leaves continually give joy as they colour in autumn, while clusters of seedheads, almost like miniature Old Man's Beard, are prominent on the tips of every drooping spray. The Beauty Bush grows strongly, requiring some pruning, but its attraction is the way its branches arch and protrude as if an artist had arranged them.

Two of these abundant shrubs so arranged in this fashion outgrew their allotted space between shrub roses, shading apple trees from essential sunlight; although they may be propagated from soft wood cuttings in the summer, they were removed with as much root as possible to new homes in the Wild Garden in early November where they can display their loveliness to the best advantage.

Larger shrub roses look their best when planted where they can layer their arching branches, without hindrance, thus displaying a wealth of fragrant flowers. Some of the more recent New English roses are recurrent flowering, making them valuable additions to our gardens. 'Cerise Bouquet', being a fairly recent introduction, is well worth growing wherever there is room, although her flowered growth requires some pruning in order that good quality flowers may develop.

Where gardens lie at high altitudes in colder areas Tea and Floribunda roses do not have so long a flowering season, but it is still well worth growing a few of these scented beauties.

Shrub roses are usually hardier, providing strongly scented flowers and often architectural qualities, fit for a painter's palette. When autumn arrives, so do quantities of brilliant hips on many varieties, particularly the species roses, such as the Chinese *Rosa 'Cantabrigiensis'*, or the fernlike *R. primula*. These all need careful pruning when they have become established. Frequently it is wise to tip back arching sprays that have become too long and wind prone, and occasionally remove some of the old wood to ground level where the centre of the shrubs have become too dense. The old roses *should* be grown on their own roots, for the history of many species roses goes back into antiquity. Long-handled pruners, about two feet in length, make an ideal Christmas present, saving one hours of back-ache, and also from being really harmed with thorns.

In these last nights, the brilliant moon has proclaimed frost. Dahlias are ruined early except where useful shrubs gave protection. It is time to safeguard young shrubs that are not altogether hardy in the North. This is where my usual wigwams of spruce branches or their like are vital to such treasures as magnolias. Visitors coming to both our gardens, particularly to Huntfield, frequently remark — "Can you really grow magnolias in such a cold garden?" Seeing is believing, and at this moment *Magnolia wilsonii* and *M. sieboldii*, each twenty-five years old, are covered with fascinating fruits that look like miniature scaly pineapples, ruby in colour, replacing exotic white flowers the shape of Chinese tea-bowls. In their earlier years, wigwams of branches were used to protect them each winter. Air, sunlight and rain penetrated, and yet this covering safeguarded their existence. Another magnolia, *M.* x *soulangeana* 'Alba Superba', was planted this spring in the Wild Garden at Dalemain, and this too will be safely cloaked each winter until its roots become firmly established.

PART III

Summer's bounteousness
becomes Autumn's fulfilment

LOVE WALKED IN

When my love walked in through the garden door
The earth was clothed in green.
Sweet song birds sang of their silvan store
Larks soared to the great unseen.

The earth refreshed from its long winter sleep
Love rose with the mists at the dawn;
Bluebells kept vigil with snowflakes to peep
While daisies danced down on the lawn.

Cherries bowed low, with their full, fragrant flowers,
Like courtiers awaiting their king
Blossoms enriched from sweet scent laden showers
For love had returned with the spring.

Love settled for tea one hot summer's day
Where roses looked down from the wall:
Meadows drift perfume of new laden hay
Pale pansies gave charm to them all.

Lilies were laughing while evenings were cool,
Lawns sparkled with pearl-studded dew;
We walked hand-in-hand by flash fisher bird's pool
Our future most close bound, we knew.

When love danced all night in rich autumn attire,
Entwining my love with his own,
My heart was alive, for the woods were on fire
With glory, for us two alone.

Soft winds whispered, rustled, and frolic'd around
Whilst love opened the woodland door.
For richness and colour of harvest abound
When earth yields her life-giving store.

Harvest rich-ripened of fields and of streams,
In garden, through devious ways:
Meadow sweets, marigolds wandered my dreams
Of love, lasting all through my days.

When love wandered in on a wild winter's morn,
His coat rustled freshly soft snow,
He held me securely from sunset to dawn
His love sure for ever I know.

When winds and fierce snow storms are blowing,
Our fireside, warmed, welcome is there
Our home is where embers are glowing
And my love is asleep in his chair.

Sweet spring returns surely, attendants in state,
High summer must follow, forbye;
But when love wandered in through the old garden gate
I knew he had claimed me for aye.

PATTERNS OF PERFECTION

August 1986

The cultivation of roses goes back to remote historical times; probably recorded first in China at least 5,000 years ago, although fossil evidence shows that distribution was much wider before historical records were kept. Their edible qualities were appreciated in early times, particularly medicinal properties of certain species.

Our well-known dog rose, *Rosa canina*, is useful to plant in hedges and so beautiful, its pale pink and occasionally white flowers become transformed into an abundance of flame-coloured hips. Many of us remember gathering these during the war to be made into rosehip syrup. Full of vitamin C, it was distributed free to all children throughout Britain. How the babies loved it! It was especially useful for children who lived in towns whose families had no gardens from which to produce all manner of nourishing fruits and vegetables.

The original wild or species roses in their various habitats would reproduce themselves freely, remaining true to type, all belonging to the northern hemisphere where they would develop along their own lines, influenced by climatic factors. It is from these truly wild roses that man, in his search for aesthetic qualities and culinary properties among plants of every kind, has gradually evolved hundreds of mutations and varieties of present-day roses.

It is readily understood that these pure roses, and their natural descendants, which differ widely according to their country of origin, grow on their own roots; by this I mean they were not grafted or budded on to other stocks in the way that modern tea roses and others are grown. For this reason, species roses never produced suckers.

It is with some sadness that I have come to realise that some nurserymen graft "old" roses to save time and to be able to send them more quickly to market, which naturally makes them a most profitable concern. It probably takes towards three years to strike cuttings of roses and to grow them on until they are sufficiently rooted to be plants in their own right. There are, of course, perfectionists who still grow shrub roses from cuttings, and it is important when building up a collection of old-fashioned species roses to be certain to buy these, otherwise endless patience will be necessary to remove strong, unwanted suckering growths.

Many years ago I bought a couple of a very attractive hybrid *rugosa* called 'Roseraie de l'Hay', a rose which was bred in 1901. It is a splendid shrub whose large, loose crimson-purple blooms open almost flat and smell of sugared almonds. But each year, strong suckers appear in the centre of these thorny bushes; and other people have told me the same story. I could not understand this until talking with a wise old nurseryman who told me the reason. The foliage of this rose, and some other *rugosas*, change to the most beautiful corn colour in autumn which makes them useful shrubs for planting as groups where space allows. The pure white hybrid *R. rugosa* 'Blanche Double de Coubert' bred in France in 1892 is one of the most beautiful, with a superb fragrance.

During the fifteenth and sixteen centuries nurserymen and rose fanciers began to cross-breed with earlier species roses: the Dutch were probably in the forefront of these enterprises and wonderful full-petalled roses are shown in their paintings as something very new and desirable.

From these mutations and other sources the most beautiful shrub roses were raised. The French were not long in playing their part, encouraged by the Empress Josephine who created her wonderful gardens at the Château de Malmaison filling it with all her favourite roses. So many of the most famous roses of this period came by chance as seedlings, or from man-made crosses. One of these, the Portland Rose, came by way of the second Duchess of Portland and thence to France, becoming the forerunner of many lasting roses. The original Bourbon rose was reared in France by M. Jacques who was head gardener to the Duc d'Orleans. He was sent seed by his friend, M Bréon, director of a small botanical garden on an island called Bourbon in the southern Indian Ocean, since renamed Reunion. On this island, at that time, roses were used as hedges. Seedling roses, grown from that present of seed, eventually became the forerunners of new Bourbon roses, still so beautiful in our own gardens.

Possibilities are endless, and it makes one's collection of "old roses" so much more interesting to attempt to understand a little of their history: otherwise it is as if one went into a library unable to read a book.

The Empress Josephine's own rose is a wonderful sight at Dalemain, growing in the long, hilly border in front of wall-trained apple trees. Its origin is thought to be *R. gallica* x *R. pendulina*; masses of double pink flowers on a free-standing bush about five feet by four feet are produced, while highlights of lavender and pale pinks add to the charm of this slightly fragrant rose.

The Emperor Napoleon married Marie Louise, daughter of the Archduke of Austria, as his second wife: her rose, c 1813, is equally beautiful, bushy and fairly free of thorns with perfumed double pink flowers, full and flat-faced when opened. I planted it near the summer house at the topmost part of the garden where it looks perfect.

Many roses of this period have relatively uncertain parentage. 'Georges Vibert' is one of these: delectably striped, the stripes are various shades of pink, carmine or purple according to the soil in which they grow. Only three feet high it is useful in limited space. 'Leda', the Painted Damask Rose is, as you may imagine, an artist's joy, its pale pink, double flowers touched with crimson markings.

One of my favourites is the larger shrub, *Rosa hugonis*, the Golden Rose of China, whose wealth of fern-like leaves turn harvest colours in autumn. Its mass of primrose flowers are the earliest to bloom at Dalemain: these are followed by a wealth of small shining blackish red hips. Growing where part of the Victorian glasshouse and its vinery once stood, this huge, graceful bush is a constant feature in our garden, besides lending shelter to little things established as ground cover beneath its spread, and especially to a wonderful *Acer palmatum* 'Senkaki', whose brilliant red shoots need protection in our uncertain climate, and to a newly planted camellia, which, so far, seems to aprove of its new home, for both the foregoing dislike an alkaline soil.

Shrub roses in their many interesting forms and manner of growth usually develop good roots. One soon learns how each type likes to be pruned in order to give of its best, and, so that one does not destroy years of bloom by careless pruning. Their exquisite beauty and perfume will repay efforts to build up a collection, a hundredfold.

COUNTRY CHILDREN

Tell me a tale of these wild border hills
Where the geese rest hidden and deep;
Tell me a story, Granny,
Of winds that will hush me to sleep.

Tell us a tale while we climb into bed
Of hills where we wander and ride
Stories to tell to our own little ones
Which they, too, will want to confide.

Of these well-watered lands of the Borders,
Of green hills that are far off, and high,
Where sunlight flits over the valleys
And wanders the wondrous blue sky.

Where the peewits call down on the farmland
And where skylarks soar through the unseen,
While a lone owl calls down in the beechwood
Where their leaves are as lace in spring green.

Of those shy moorland birds in the heather
Where red grouse cry "do get away back"
Of the young wounded deer in the dawning
Or a fox on a snow covered track.

A story of springs on the hillside
That gather together and flow
Into fast flowing, rich, rippling waters
Replenished with bountiful snow.

Of a boy who goes out on the farmland
To the pond, with his rod and a reel
With a ball which is lost in the bushes
And a dear little dog at his heel.

Or the tale of a fine grey pony
And a girl with streaming gold hair
Riding the wealth of the morning
The freedom of fresh mountain air.

BLESSINGS OF PEACE

September 1989

We were always told in past days that an eclipse brought unsettled weather, and this was certainly the case after the perfect eclipse of the moon on August 17th. The sky was clear when the full moon was transformed into a glowing reddish globe, but the earth still yearned for rain; two days later wild winds were driving welcome rain across the hills: straw that had yet to be gathered, and dust from corn fields blew and tumbled in unaccustomed weather. Half an inch of rain fell at Dalemain that Sunday, August 20th.

What a relief to see border flowers raising their heads to meet intermittent sun. Mallard, teal and waterhens sailed happily on fast flowing waters: baby swallows, perched on window sills, waited patiently to be fed: soon after, rows of young ones gathered on telegraph lines; surely it is very early for these migrants to prepare to fly their long perilous journey. Last October, late families were still assembling for their unseen flight. How can we, who love creatures of the wild, ever teach people in foreign lands to value these birds of passage and so many others, instead of netting and destroying our harbingers of spring. My customary family of swallows are still busy in the potting shed.

Long grass in the Wild Garden was cut after daffodils had wilted; rough herbage full of unwanted seeds raked up and burnt: since then it has been possible to go over most of the same ground with the small tractor mower, cutting awkward places with a strimmer, once more raking up and removing mowings. If this is done for a third time, a much better, lawn-like surface makes it possible for finer grasses and wild flowers to seed and germinate. It is the lazy man's way out to let cuttings lie to rot, for only rough herbage, hogweeds and the like will be able to penetrate the folly of ungathered mowings.

Through improved surfaces autumn crocus and late treasures will be able to emerge, for their flower buds are safely below the surface until September, giving of their luminous beauty until finally put to sleep by consistent frosts. Plant these colchicums in early spring in sheltered, moist places where they will spread, making an unexpected show just as so many inhabitants of the garden are ready to go to sleep. The waterlily type, with faces just as you would expect from the name, are particularly lovely, but more expensive. I find they flower even longer than the usual species. Other species crocus, flowering at this time of year, spread happily: they, like so many little bulbs or corms, enjoy gritty homes.

The dry summer has taught us much about plants which survive drought conditions and others one should establish for the future. The Terrace border at Dalemain, as usual, takes the brunt of hot weather with high walls reflecting heat: on one occasion when weeding and removing Sticky Willie before this horror seeds prolifically, heat from the soil was so great on my face that I had to give up.

Agapanthus, the blue Lilies of the Nile, have been wonderful: they seem to thrive in heat and droughty conditions. Hardy varieties growing in large clumps are still producing a wealth of blooms: some are ready to divide in order to create further successful groups along this border: with plenty of rotted manure around their surface they bloom unfailingly. The larger, half-hardy *A. umbellatus*, grown in 9-inch pots and sunk in dull corners among silver and variegated plants, have also made a wonderful show.

Biggar's Flower Show encourages children to bring their treasures. Enchanting miniature gardens attract many entries. When David was ten years old, he decided to make a winter garden, around a little house amongst lovely bits and pieces off woodland floors: a tiny goods train with logs and milk churns journeyed at the far end, while the whole scene was covered in "snow". It won a special! Even Hermione, aged two and a half, made a garden with a pond and mosses and tiny flower heads which she picked, mostly off the lawn! I was anxious to transport a salmon-coloured standard fuchsia — but how to get it safely to the show? So I sat in the back of the Subaru pick-up, holding up the stem with one hand and supporting the large pot on its side with my feet. Hermione insisted on coming with me, so with my free arm round the little girl to keep her safe, the van rattled round corners to the Show. We arrived intact with all our treasures! These little people must be encouraged, for they are the gardeners of future years. My salmon-coloured fuchsia won first prize; the ticket proudly remains in our potting shed.

How lucky we were to be able to hold our Show once more, on the same day on which that terrible war broke out fifty years ago. So truly fortunate that our land can enjoy *freedom*, and *peace* — those wonderful words, ensuring the continuation and friendship of flower shows all over our islands, instead of the necessity of Digging for Victory.

Hermione

David

Saya

Robert Bolton & Co's new Sweet Peas, 1991, 'Dalemain' (above) and 'Sylvia Mary'

FOR CHARLES AND PETER

Born September 1989 and December 1990

I'm just a little toddler,
The youngest of us three
I'm David's faithful shadow
And Saya's good to me.

She takes me on her pony
And never lets me fall
But since David plays in every team
I'm always playing ball.

But now I'm not the youngest
For there's Peter in my bed
So it's time I started morning school
And learnt to draw instead.

EARLY MORNING FANTASIES

October 1988

October mornings are slow to waken, but I love to gaze from our bathroom window upon trees of many sorts attired in flamboyant colours of their autumn robes. Being an early riser, having heard so often from childhood days that the best hours are before breakfast, I am eager to watch while those mysterious minutes slip away and day-light begins to fall on the world outside. In these some-what misty mornings trees take on illusions of fantasy. That wonderful butter-coloured maple, *Acer cappadocicum*, which I planted thirty years ago in the Woodland Garden outside the house, lost its leader in an earlier gale and appears to me like a young girl in a Georgian ball-gown in this half light, her tiered skirt of auburn hue taking on the colour of burnt gold, similar to those patches of soft russet gold grass that help to carpet grassy hillsides along the upper reaches of Tweed; colours which never cease to give us yet another thrill on our regular journeys between Huntfield and Dalemain.

Those stately Edwardian ladies with large hats, narrow necks and bustled dresses in the pony field are strong growing sycamores, trees that were frequently planted or self-sown close to farm steadings on both sides of the Borders. They give tremendous shelter and are firm rooted, as opposed to lacy-like ash trees which worried my Father when growing too close to buildings. Scots pines, standing like sentinels in the mists — such beautiful trees when planted in groups on a hillside. Hemlock spruces with wide flowing skirts in frills like ballet dancers. Five-fingered horse-chestnut leaves falling like gold in the winds — give one to a tiny child to hold up, like a fan, and they will never forget. This is how I try to teach our grandchildren about the trees, so that trees become a real and necessary part of their lives — the love of trees of all sorts and sizes which protect our homes, our countryside from gales, build up nourishment in the good earth which gives back its goodness a hundredfold if we care for it properly.

So many little creatures benefit from leafy homes in the winter, creatures that do so much good; spiders are clean creatures and black beetles eat slugs that ruin our plants.

Now the dawn has broken and sunshine falls on a wealth of foliage. There is no need for our gardens to be dull in winter when flowers give up their battle against the elements. Plants with variegated foliage are well worth cultivating. Variegated figworts, a member of the phygelius family, have been greatly admired in both our gardens. These soon form good plants with plenty of cream and dark green foliage, while marvellous young growth forms a colourful skirt. A small variety of the Umbrella Plant, peltiphyllum, growing in our garden, has a wealth of brilliant flame decorative leaves, sheltering a clump of a late-flowering double-pink meadowsweet; but the glory of herbaceous borders at this late season is *Sedum* 'Autumn Joy', with wide heads of salmon pink, always changing in colour with wild days of scurrying lights and shadows. Its smaller relation, *S.* 'Ruby Glow', is more suitable for smaller spaces. I plant daffodils of differing shapes and sizes amongst these useful plants, giving early colour amongst late herbaceous flowers.

This year hardy agapanthus are a glory in themselves at present, having withstood that harsh frost on September 29/30th. When their large plants are divided they soon make good clumps; they are planted in sunniest positions, but at Huntfield some are planted in more exposed places to bring colour and interest to borders near the house, and still survive happily; they enjoy plenty of farm manure in early spring; leafmould is an added benefit when spread round them before Christmas; their startling blue, lily type of flowers look exotic behind floriferous sedums.

The well-tried *Clematis* x *jackmanii* should never be forgotten; its long lasting purple flowers are peeping into our kitchen window, their elegant stems and buds like a watercolour painting; climbing up a herringbone *Cotoneaster horizontalis*, it has adequate support. Brilliant tropaeoleum, the Scots creeper, also takes advantage of this position, eventually losing quantities of red petals behind which have formed blue-black seeds, eventually falling into gravel below. Here they like to settle, and can be lifted in early spring to form new colonies. Tropaeoleum only likes to be moved with some of the soil in which it is growing. When I was a child it grew profusely on the yew hedge sheltering the Knot Garden, and after many years of neglect and hedge cutting at the wrong moment, they disappeared, unable to form seeds for future generations. Gradually plants from our hospitable pebbled gravel are taking up their renewed residence across the Border.

FESTIVAL OF FLOWERS

October 1985

"What wonderful colour you still have in your gardens," visiting enthusiasts constantly remark, "and what a variety of plants are still flowering to perfection despite all this dreadful wet weather."

I can't help but laugh at their amazement, for there are so many plants, shrubs, and bulbs too, that are easily available and which will bring joy and variation to the smallest or the largest gardens all the year round. A garden is not a thing of beauty for summertime alone. I attempt to explain to friends and casual visitors that we try to have something in bloom every single week of the year, unless of course plant life is safely tucked up beneath a life-saving blanket of snow, happily out of the reach of searing winds.

If December should be a reasonably mild month, a few golden aconites are often dancing with delight in sheltered places around Christmas time, heralding the concourse of their friends and relatives that will bloom with snowdrops, and the first crocus, forerunners of many to flower in the weeks ahead.

Earlier in December the last of autumn flowers are frequently bringing much wanted colour, unless frost has taken its toll of easily damaged blooms. Roses can still be flowering at this late date, and some varieties are particularly hardy: *R.* 'Iceberg', being one of the most reliable, while 'All Gold', 'Arthur Bell', 'Silver Jubilee' are a few more of those which have stood up regularly to bad weather conditions. That wonderful vermilion red Hybrid tea rose, Alexander, causes quite a sensation near the summer-house at the top of the hill in our garden; since this rose grows tall for its type, it impels one to look and admire its glowing, lamp-like beauty on late autumn days.

Border phloxes have been particularly good this year, since they revel in damp conditions and even after a really wet night they remain standing straight and colourful. *P.* 'Silver Salmon', pinky-lilac, is one of my favourites, and *P.* 'Dresden China' another. 'Brigadier', a fine cherry, has stood the test of time; 'White Admiral's' large shapely head and sweet-scented 'Lavender Dream' are all worth growing: perhaps the best of all is 'Franz Schubert', a magnificent, sturdy, pale lilac with wonderful rich fragrance. Phloxes require to be divided regularly in order to produce large heads of quality, otherwise the centres of the plants cannot breathe, becoming woody and useless.

Visitors look with amazement upon great clumps of agapanthus, each producing quantities of rich blue flowers on long strong stems above a bevy of fine strap-like leaves. Blue is so often thought of as the time of bluebells or perhaps *Cynoglossum nervosum* whose gentian blue tubular flower heads decorate summer borders, emerging freely from among rough, hairy leaves.

Then, suddenly, as autumn dawns, borders are filled with these exotic looking blue Lilies of the Nile. There are, of course, the larger growing varieties too, which are so useful planting in nine-inch pots, where they can stand in dull corners of the garden or decorate a pool; but these must be kept under cover before frosts arrive.

Herbaceous agapanthus have withstood many winters in both our gardens and benefit greatly from being divided every three years or so; probably it is better to do this in early spring since they expend their energy so late in the year. At the present moment they are absolutely beautiful, a riot of colour. One is advised to cover their crowns in winter with branches, bracken or the like, but this has been unnecessary in our experience.

Nearby, contrasting with the agapanthus, groups of snowy-white bladder campions, *Silene barbata*, make a worth-while show. Easy to establish and long-lived, these unusual herbaceous plants sprawl about the border lifting stems some two feet high, each covered with a multitude of eye-catching flowers in truly ornamental fashion.

Growing in sheltered places or half climbing against sunny walls, *Phygelius capensis* makes a splendid wealth of colour; masses of scarlet trumpet-shaped flowers clothe countless semi-woody stems with glory above an abundance of blue-green foliage. Easily propagated from plentiful runners, this South African beauty has spent more than thirty winters quite safely in our gardens. Chinese lanterns, *Physalis alkekengi franchettii*, are easy customers too; not only are they colourful, but their lantern-like flowers dry well for winter decoration: they revel in sunny situations, especially where their roots can expand among gravel on the edge of a path, but they do appreciate a mulch in early spring. All these herbaceous plants are worthy of room space, and provided they are given a feed of farm manure, leaf mould, or general fertiliser before growth actually appears to be on the upsurge, they will provide interest and a wealth of colour at this late season of the year.

OCTOBER RAIN

Raindrops falling on my eyes
While I gaze up to the skies
Dark'ning clouds go gliding past
For autumn's chill is here at last.

Raindrops falling on my nose
While shortening back that lovely rose,
Pruning ramblers on the wall
Is not a rapid work at all.

Raindrops patter on the leaves
Where busy magic spider weaves
Webs of most fantastic lace
In patterns, placed, with utmost grace.

Raindrops while I gaze and dream
And sing myself a different theme
Of skylarks on a sunset hill
Where peewits add another thrill

Now raindrops tumble down my coat
The colour of an ermine stoat
It surely must be time to stay
And leave it for a warmer day.

November 1988

FORGOTTEN TREASURES

October 1987

Have you ever grown meadow saffrons, those enchanting corms which flower in profusion at this time of the year? Creating long-lived magic carpets, they are still a joy in many corners of our two gardens — lilac flowers, illuminated with autumn sunshine lighting their upturned faces. Nearby, sheltering *Berberis thunbergii* glows like ripening corn, while dark-leaved hazel and coppery-purple berberis reflect contrasting colours to these lilac beauties.

Autumn Crocus, the name commonly given to these saffrons, native of Swiss and other meadowlands, differ from true crocuses in having six and not three stamens; they are also known as Naked Ladies, since glossy leaves appear in March, then die down, until suddenly in late August white-lilac buds push upwards when one had almost forgotten they were there at all. Charming double water-lily varieties are particularly beautiful, as well as the many single varieties. Grow them amongst sweet woodruff which smells of new-mown hay, and other ground-cover so that there is always colour and interest. Woodruff can be clipped back just before these colchicums arise from their underworld in early September, if one remembers to do this in time — Colchis an ancient part of Asia Minor from where these lilac beauties originated.

True autumn crocus, both bright violet-blue *C. speciosus* and lavender *C. zonatus*, flower about the same time. Although they grow in grass, they are happiest when planted in drier situations, being flowers of the Middle East. They seed readily in gravel on the edge of the Terrace border at Dalemain, and although forgotten when herbaceous plants possess the border, they arise again with shining morning faces, asking that stronger neighbours now past their best, should be cut back or removed.

It is my ambition to grow hardy cyclamen in plentiful numbers which like to settle under trees or in any shady position where they will not be disturbed, and where the ground does not become weedy. Some years ago I planted a few corms of the pale pink *C. neapolitanum* beneath a golden berberis where a few emerge faithfully each September. The loveliest hardy cyclamen I have ever seen are pure white, growing among knobbly roots of a huge elm tree, on a lawn at Broughton Place near Biggar, whilst at Levens, in Westmorland, a wondrous carpet of pink cyclamen flower unfailingly beneath a topiary yew tree which is clipped about eighteen inches all round the trunk to clear the ground. In these extremely dry conditions they grow well, for in such places as Cyprus they grow along roadsides like our own wild flowers. They *can* be grown successfully from seed, but are best planted in growing condition, if obtainable.

To grow so many bulbs, and also perennial flowers, one must understand their native conditions to enable them to grow successfully. Do they like to grow in cool, shady conditions which never dry out, or are they sunlovers which require the warmest places in our gardens? One cannot say "choicest places" for there are lists of plants and bulbs which will more than fill every corner of our gardens, whether it be a hardy morello cherry to flower profusely on a sunless, north-facing wall, or a succulent eating apple, or Victoria plum to plant with anticipation and pleasure on our sunniest wall.

Clematis is a most useful and attractive perennial, available in many forms. They all like to grow with their feet in shade where they can ramble up into sunshine. One of the fascinating *Clematis flammula*, better known as the Virgin's Bower was planted against an archway crossing a shady grass path; its numerous sprays of fragrant white flowers ramble at will, each recurving petal shaded blue, revealing a boss of yellow anthers. Sprays of this richly fragrant clematis are delightful to gather and use in a pedestal arrangement of flowers in the house; it is a joy to walk beneath the archway and gaze at the profusion of star-like flowers.

There are so many glorious flowers still blooming in mid-October — dahlias, heliotrope, cosmea, gentians, and agapanthus. Why not plan to grow something unusual in your garden next autumn, which will be admired by all who pass your way?

AT HOME WITH MRS MOUSE

Under the old oak staircase
You can see such a quaint little house,
With tiny brass knocker and doorway,
Which belongs to an old-fashioned mouse.

There's always a fire in her chimney,
For children play games on the floor,
While she sits with her specs and her knitting,
Lamplight glowing bright 'neath the door.

Babies are rocked in their cradles,
'Cause "early to bed" is her rule;
Toddlers are doing their homework
While teenagers run off to school.

Often she's doing her shopping,
For Cook spills good food on the floor:
That kitchen's a wonderful market
And up in the nursery, there's more.

Choice little plants in the greenhouse,
Seeds neatly set out in a line;
Mrs Mouse feasts with her basket
So long as the weather is fine.

Mr Mouse helps with the housework;
He likes to go shopping as well.
When they're all home by the fireside,
I surely, never can tell.

April 1991

LADIES IN WAITING

November 1982

Not many Sundays past the text for the sermon was taken from the Book of Isaiah . . . "there shall come forth a rod out of the stem of Jesse and a Branch shall grow out of his roots." Day-dreaming as usual, among fields and gardens and in the realms of horticulture, my ears pricked up at these words, and I immediately thought of my buddleja trees which were at that very moment breaking into strong green growth close to the base of the saddened main trunk. Until recently, they, like many other of our flowering shrubs, appeared to be dead, the winter having been too severe for some of our supposedly hardy old friends. To my joy, one day, when wandering to the top of the garden at Dalemain — my eyes always alert for the unusual, or for good seedlings which ought to be nurtured — I saw that the white buddleja growing in the Children's garden beside the doorway into Lobb's Wood was breaking into abundant growth. With a little prayer of thankful happiness I hurried on to look at similar shrubs, supposedly dead, and was overjoyed to see the large *Escallonia* 'Appleblosom' breaking all the way along the old wood.

During the months that have elapsed since those severe weeks of late frosts, I have continually preached the gospel of *waiting* to other gardeners; do not be in a hurry to cut down valued shrubs and flowering trees that have suffered cruelly. The will to live is very strong, and it is a wise gardener who bides his time to give the plant world time to recover. Climbing roses too were sorely stricken. On the Terrace walk where Rambler and *wichuraiana* roses grow as bushes, their long arching growths pegged in places to the gravel which covers the defensive walls of the medieval tower, new shoots which will flower next year are rising above the browned branches; this dead wood is being gradually cut away, but in the meantime it is useful to protect the soft young growth from prevailing winds that blow down the Ullswater valley and even stronger winds blowing from Blencathra, Skiddaw and the Borrowdale heights. The beautiful 'Easlea's Golden Rambler' was hit the worst of all the roses along the Terrace. For many years it was one of the glories of June, covering a wide circle on the gravel where it trails its scented, blossom-laden branches in profusion. Not since the terrible war winter of 1941 have these roses been stricken so badly. After that winter, which only seems like yesterday, they had to be entirely replaced and the Terrace looked strangely bare, though quite imposing, for the remaining years of war and destruction.

This autumn it has been a wonderful open season for taking cuttings as wood ripens and hardens. It is surprising how economically one can garden if a little time and fore-thought is given to this simple art of propagating. When I was a child, and William Stuart was head gardener, a post he ably filled for more than fifty years, there were always frames filled with cuttings which produced strong short-jointed early plants the following spring. A few rows of the old lilac coloured *Viola* 'Maggie Mott' were dibbled into a sandy loam beside border carnations, penstemons and many other treasures. Stuart taught me so much. As a little girl I followed him round, watching and asking questions, frequently sitting on a wooden box in his potting shed. I would see him sow the sweet peas, or pot up Arum lilies to bloom in time for Easter, or those beautiful winter flowering begonias, *B.* Gloire de Lorraine; the clean red pots were stood on river gravel in the "hot house." They were such happy days. Up in the rafters of his potting shed, where I now attempt to emulate his skills, swallows have never failed to nest and rear their young, still returning to build in the same places as they did so many years ago, continuing to bring joy and happiness, as they dart in and out of the open door above my head, or through some unobtrusive hole in the rough walls. They never fail to thrill one's whole being, and it is the same feeling of excitement and wonder with which one gazes upon the first seedlings to germinate after the turn of the year, or when the corn is brairding across the brown furrows, or an "old friend" growing in the garden, stirs with life once more.

Old-fashioned and shrub roses are among my favourites, and many of these root very easily if the cuttings are dipped into rooting powder — such a helpful modern invention — and popped into slit trenches into which sharp sand has been added, and, most important, well trodden in before the job is concluded. These roses are grown on their own roots, so will not produce suckers. Quite a number of flowering shrubs are also easy to strike, such as forsythias, dogwoods, deutzias, and lilacs, particularly if they are "taken with a heel." But another word of warning; the following year they will only *begin* to grow into plants in their own right; even lavender cuttings, grown in a cold frame, will not be ready to lift until the summer is half-way through. They may look as if they are growing on top, but below the surface little or no root system will have formed. As for the roses, it will be another spring before they are ready to be put into their flowering quarters.

So why not "have a go"; it is exciting to "wait and see", and a lesson in patience. Raising your own plants is such fun.

WILD GEESE A-FLYING

"Hurry, Granny, listen, hurry!"
The wild geese are flying
Over muddy stubble fields
As evening lights are dying,
Flying fast in firm formation
Birds most loved of God's creation.

Listen to their wondrous chatter
As they sail above the trees,
Dark green pines and bare-leaved beechwoods
Clothed in winter's frost and freeze.
Skies are rosy, golden, clear
While pink-foot geese fly ever near.

"Hurry, Granny, stand and listen,"
Hark that sound for which you fret.
The children gaze in awesome wonder
Locked in dreams they'll ne'er forget
Holding hands, three hearts are ringing.
Bells in Heaven, where birds are singing.

Soon the geese will sleep on waters
Darkly quiet and undisturbed;
Peaty pools or lonesome lochans
Where shy brown deer graze unperturbed.
Dancing dawn reflects the sky —
"Look up, my loves, the geese ride high!"

Written for David and Saya
February 1988

QUIET AFTER STORM

November 1987

November evenings, quiet and still after these terrifying storms and floods, particularly the storm on Sunday October 18th. This happened to be the last day when Dalemain was open to visitors for the season, when Robert and I shepherded visitors through the old cow byre to their cars, the floods being so deep across the road behind the stable which is their usual route. It was frightening walking along the Terrace, for a tremendous roar of water sounded as if it was pouring through garden walls from higher ground beyond the Deer Park. In reality, it was the noise of Dacre's Beck in torrent, sweeping across the Wild Garden in tremendous force. Young trees swayed perilously while plant life was scarcely visible, only the heads of the tallest senecios appearing like ballet dancers moving upon the waters. Garden seats had to be rescued from disappearing down the Beck; one of them fortunately became lodged in an old lilac.

We were lucky compared to southern counties. A few days later floods began to recede, but gardens were too wet to work.

For some time past pink-foot geese had returned from summer feeding grounds in the far north to winter in a less harsh climate. They fly in large numbers right overhead at Huntfield from daytime feeding grounds, frequenting stubble fields close to heather-covered hills not far above the garden. As the light begins to fail, that wondrous music of their ceaseless chatter comes nearer and nearer until strong-winged geese fly steadily into view, outlined against skies of sea-green and gold set between banks of rolling cloud which artists yearn to paint. On they fly, to sleep in some quiet watery place, returning to their accustomed paths when morning fills the sky with light.

David and Saya, our two small grandchildren, are fast becoming bird-watchers. "Quick, Granny," they call when at home for weekends, "Come quickly, the geese are coming!" and we stare together watching their powerful leader command the flight. Or perhaps these children hear a scolding wren, angrily telling us that we have disturbed her nest, or we watch small gatherings of fieldfares and redwings flitting between stunted beech trees on the hill, before darting on to rough white grass cushioning remains of flower seeds and small berries; these birds make the most extraordinary harsh calls as they move, like hand clappers which children revolve at parties; here and there on the same hillsides small groups of black-faced sheep graze unperturbed, looking their best at this season of the year.

It is so important to encourage small children to watch for the wonders of the countryside and learn to understand their different ways of life; hedgehogs finding cosy places to wrap themselves in hibernation, and many other little miracles. Frequently grandparents have more time to unfold these seasonal happenings than busy parents, and what an unforgettable joy it is to be able to have the company of young enquiring minds. Even when very small, little ones love to be lifted up to touch leaves that move, or watch bantams scratching and clucking; it is a wonder in itself when complete delight streams across a baby's face. Children never forget.

When I was very small, I remember being carried by my first Nanny to watch farmyard geese strutting across the rough green outside the back door, where game larders perched on stilts beneath enormous sycamore trees. I can still hear the raucous noise the geese enjoyed making as they proudly paraded with beaks pointing to the sky.

Later, Grandfather and I wandered across fields, searching in rushy places for curlews' nests, while peewits rose from rough grass, their clear call ringing out far down the valley. Amongst rushy places, pale pink flowers of Lady's Smock grew, ideal for a child to gather — *Our* Lady's Smock, grandfather always added, for he was a very holy man and everything growing in the countryside, to him, had some religious association — the seasons of the year, little summer breezes that rise from nowhere; it was from Grandfather that I learnt to understand some of the mysteries of the countryside.

In the whitewashed farmhouse up on the hillside, safely out of frequently flooded swamps, John Howe and his wife resided. We were always welcome in their cosy kitchen at Park House. The table in their parlour was inevitably covered with a green velour embroidered cloth, while glass-fronted cupboards were filled with fascinating pieces of china and nick-nacks which will always be stored in my memory.

Before November disappears once more with starlit frosty evenings, bulbs of many sorts should be safely planted — tulips and daffodils, six inches deep, for they soon rise close to the surface for predators to destroy. Planted carefully, even most varieties of tulips will multiply to make colourful displays in future years. Miniature *Iris reticulata* are most attractive, the gentian blue variety so beautiful in early March: pale blue scillas and miniature bulbs of many sorts. If planted among rock plants where they will not be disturbed when forking among stronger growing plants, they will have a chance to settle and multiply. Catmint makes an excellent ground cover for tulips which bring colour to such a border early in the season.

We have been fortunate in the North not be be afflicted by those terrible gales, but these were a warning to see that young standard trees in our own gardens are properly staked while there is still time. If one's garden is exposed to the elements, plant hedge-like subjects on windward perimeters to catch the blast of future gales. Where alders, hazels and such-like had been used, they did much to protect many gardens. They are hardy and beautiful in their own right, alders bearing shining leaves and copious yellow catkins, while an occasional purple-leaved hazel, planted here and there, brings delightful contrast. Dogwoods are equally good, available in many varieties, their coloured stems creating ornamental thickets; available in many varieties, *Cornus alba* 'Sibirica' produces brilliant red shoots bringing colour to the garden in winter time.

PART IV

The later months when plant
life prepares to rest.

ST LUKE'S LITTLE SUMMER

Where do you come from
Wild winds of the west?
Join with your brothers
Chill winds from the east.

October's our Maytime
While autumn's our playtime
We'll billow and buffet and sing as we go
Till lost in high hills amongst first flakes of snow.

Under arched bridges
White waters of Tweed,
Struggling white horses with power in your limbs
Mythical horses, some fairy tale's steed.
Night will turn frost-filled, but now you have fun,
Magical horses awake in the sun.

Up in the marshes
Bent grasses lie low
Hillsides stand staunchly
Where roughly you go;
Heathers and harebells
Are things of the past,
St Luke's Little Summer
Is dancing at last.

October 1990

Black Irises at Dalemain

Garden gate, Huntfield

Terrace Border, Dalemain

Easlea's Golden Rambler

ST. LUKE'S CAPRICIOUS SUMMER

November 1985

It was the last Sunday in October, the day when summer time ends and daylight draws to a close, even more rapidly when clocks are put back by one hour. Previous days were filled with storm; gale force winds swirled with relentless ferocity, tearing foliage from trees and tumbling colourful late-flowering herbaceous plants.

It was a cruel end to autumn's glory. Lengthy young shoots of climbing roses swayed perilously unless previously tied to supporting wires. While these develop, especially during our late summer, it is imperative to arrange them securely in position, and at the same time to cut back their growing points; this action will force them to send out flowering shoots from leaf axils down the length of strong healthy shoots which, if left untied, are at so much risk in stormy weather — it is these which will provide next summer's display of scented loveliness.

While walking along the Terrace at Dalemain in fearful trepidation while the storm still raged, my eyes were somehow averted from Swarth Fell's blustery heights to the long herbaceous border beside the gravel walk where the glory of golden rudbeckias filled my vision with delight; instead of standing upright, their green conelike centres pointing to the sky, they had bent over gracefully in the wrath of the gale, appearing as a waterfall of delight along the entire length of the border, intermingled with tall clover-coloured Michaelmas daisies and stately coral coloured plume poppies, *Macleaya microcarpa*, whose grey-green, lobed leaves, grey-white beneath, are an ornament in themselves. Tall black spires of *Cimicifuga racemosa*, known as Bugwort, still formed large statuesque groups, each spire clothed in soft white cloud-like flowers, again with eye-catching leaves. These long-lasting herbaceous plants are useful, reliable, old-fashioned plants which give of their best despite all types of autumnal weather until it is long past the time to cut down and tidy up.

The Terrace is a splendid place to grow rambling roses in bush form along the edge of the ha-ha wall; long growths are arched on to the gravel by arranging small hoops of fencing wire over the tips of these branches, the hoops pushed securely into the gravel walk. Some branches hang freely down the ha-ha above the Low Garden. This former eighteenth-century garden is now a sheltered meadow where sheep can safely graze. Such special well-watered meadows have long since been called "Paradise Fields" in the Border country, particularly in Northumberland; this name gives the feeling of complete peacefulness.

Rambling roses had recently been pruned, much of the old wood cut to the ground, while those of Tea rose type had their long branches shortened and dead wood removed. It never ceases to make me wonder at the resurgence of nature, causing these hard cut Ramblers to produce unlimited new growths each summer. Of course they must be fed; bone meal in the autumn provides a long-lived source of nourishment followed by well rotted farm manure. Later planted roses must be well trodden in to prevent rocking in gales.

When the border is cut down and well cleaned, large clumps of herbaceous plants will be lifted, divided and replanted where possible; dividing old plants enables them to produce much better flowers and foliage. The border is forked, but not usually dug, thus avoiding root damage, and possibly the loss of unexpected precious seedlings which may appear from unknown sources. The front of this long border is a mass of low growing, semi-prostrate plants protecting hundreds of bulbs which multiply at will, including fragile autumn crocus in lovely shades of blues and lilacs and in the spring, grape hyacinths, Stars of Bethlehem and tulips which prefer to be left undisturbed.

Down the stone staircase built into the end of the Terrace wall, I went into the Wild Garden, formerly part of the Low Garden; here Dacre's Beck was in full flood, its torrent of brown water risen provocatively overnight; but, lo! in the shelter of the steep, tree-covered bank, *Viburnum fragrans*, was already covered with sweet smelling pink flowers, and would remain so until April. What a wonderful shrub, worthy of a place in any garden; the species has pale, pink, tubular flowers, while the Bodnant variety has flowers of a deeper hue which are shown to advantage against its display of dark, deeply veined leaves. Carry a sprig into the house to scent your room and bring you joy. It was as if this winter-flowering viburnum in all its glory was saying "Never despair, wait and see what tomorrow morning will bring."

THE CHARM OF BLUE POPPIES

October 1988

I was amazed to read in a reliable magazine that meconopsis were not reliably perennial, particularly the well tried *M. Baileyi* (*M. Betonicifolia*). This was the first "blue poppy" to be discovered.

It was certainly the first Himalayan poppy to be grown in our garden at Huntfield thirty years ago when I was introduced to these treasures by Jack Drake of Aviemore. Large clumps of this wonderful plant grow happily under harsh winter conditions. These conditions are probably ideal, for plants of all sorts never dry out, even in our occasional droughtiest spells of summer, but my three original plants and their offspring never faltered. Some of them were moved to our garden at Dalemain in Cumbria in different soil and only 400 feet above sea level. These, too, formed strong perennial plants, rejoicing under the protection of snowfalls.

Meconopsis, of all the species and hybrids since grown, appreciate well rotted farmyard manure and leafmould to give them the cool well-fed conditions they enjoy. I find it is much easier to lift and divide some of the large plants when further stocks are needed, than to grow from seed, though some seedlings appear; these are carefully nurtured, some surviving to flowering status, since one always hopes to be lucky enough to find a new colour break.

Blue poppies enthrall me with their loveliness; to gaze out of our bedroom windows at Huntfield upon these miracles of blue, growing at random in groups in the woodland garden beyond the house, and close to the kitchen and sun parlour, is utter joy; light and shade fall playfully upon their petals, reflecting and varying colours of spring and summer skies.

I have grown to recognise, even from our windows, the various meconopsis which are now established happily in our two gardens, each species or hybrid kept somewhat separate from the others.

George Sheriff's *M. grandis* is the most magnificent of all with strong stems and rich blue flowers, richer than all the others. Its leaves form canopies of foliage, through which only an occasional persistent creeping buttercup can penetrate. He discovered this beauty in 1938 on his last visit to the Himalayas and grew them on in his garden in Fife. On the same expedition Mrs Sheriff had a dream that she would find a pink meconopsis; she left the others to clear up their camp and in a little while, there they were — her dream had come true! These pink meconopsis seem very difficult to establish, but John Lawson, Jack's follower, is persevering with this intrepid customer.

One blue poppy gives me particular satisfaction, for it was discovered by grandfather's old friend, Cicely Crewdson, who lived near Kendal. I was impelled to buy three plants and attempt to discover their source, the plants grew well, and multiplied, their strong stems somewhat greener blue than *M. grandis* GS600 and their longer pointed leaves more upright with an auburn hue to their somewhat furry reverse sides. It is a lovely poppy.

Sure enough, when I was recovering from meningitis, an unexpected visitor arrived at Dalemain to see me. This was none other than Cicely's daughter, Nancy Jones, who lived in nearby Mungrisedale. She was so excited to find that her mother's favourite "break" was growing, trouble-free, in both our gardens. She thought it had been lost long ago. On her next visit, she brought her mother's scrap-book which I browsed through at leisure, seeing old photographs of her mother, winning more than one award from the Royal Horticultural Society. I so well remember Cicely coming to Dalemain, my childhood home when I was a small girl, to take tea with our family, but especially with Grandfather, for they were old friends. My recollections are of Cicely wearing long skirts and a hat with pearly hat pins, while her hair was pinned up beneath, for I sat beside her, listening entranced to their talk about plants, Grand-father being a keen plantsman too.

About a month ago, among a bed of really blue *M. grandis*, I spied two plants, clothed with clovery-pink blooms. Always looking for a "break", this seemed really exciting, so long as the much wanted colour remains stable in years ahead. Canes were pushed into the ground beside these two, or possibly three, strong young plants, with twine wound between the canes: they were growing in a little group near a huge *Rosa moyesii* whose fern-like foliage and flame-coloured flagon-shaped hips looked glorious against October's hurrying skies.

The clover-coloured meconopsis have remained the same unusual colour for the two following summers, and next autumn they must be divided and replanted with great care. In our wonderful soil, it is quite amazing how even the smallest piece, broken off inadvertently, takes root, eventually becoming a good plant.

Surely, blue poppies are soundly perennial when they are capable of surviving the unheeded passing of time in our two gardens, one hundred miles apart. Both gardens give me tremendous pleasure: so much joy comes from attempting to grow and understand the needs of their various inhabitants, in order that they can thrive to give pleasure in their own abundant happiness.

FOR HERMIONE

Golden headed little one
With sunlight in your hair,
Eyes that shine with pleasure
Outside in the morning air.

Come with me my darling
And we will watch and see
The world of woodland wonders, —
P'raps a squirrel, up a tree.

We wander on the flagstones
Beside rough ancient wall
Where fairest, fairy ferns abide,
The gentlest flowers of all.

She put her hands outstretched to feel
This maidenhair-like treasure,
And next, the drooping oak-leaved fern,
Her eyes awake with pleasure.

From these we wandered hand in hand
Those cosy, leaf-strewn, secret ways
To dangle legs on garden seat
As if this was the day of days.

For me, a mem'ry, clear and mild
This peace of Sunday after church
A darling, unspoilt, country child.

November 1988

OLD ROSES

November 1990

Whenever the weather is reasonable at the present time, I am endeavouring to prune my varied collection of shrub and old-fashioned roses. Each bush must be treated as an individual, for they all have characteristics and habits of their own.

Many years ago my interest was awakened when Father's Oxford friend, Professor Cecil Morrison who was staying with us, was astounded that so few "old" shrub roses grew in Dalemain's centuries old garden. Later, he sent cuttings to me of *R. sericea pteracanta* from his own garden in Dorset. This tall handsome shrub whose young stems are covered with brilliant cherry-red, translucent thorns, catches every gleam of sunlight, but of these beware — they make an impenetrable barrier; the snow white flowers, the shape of anemones, are very decorative in early summer. Cecil Morrison also sent cuttings of *R.* 'The Garland', a vigorous climber, flowering in great profusion, with masses of semi-double daisy-like flowers, creamy white with attractive yellow stamens and delicious fragrance. These can be used to garland walls or grown through yew trees with great effect.

My interest was truly awakened and my eyes alerted for "old fashioned's" wherever we went; many strike easily from cuttings or else they produce "suckers" in the manner of raspberries; when severed from the parent plant these soon form flowering plants in their own right.

R. gallica officinalis, the Apothecary's Rose, also known as the Red Rose of Lancaster, is one of these suckering roses, with dark greyish-green foliage; light crimson semi-double flowers are highly scented and were much valued by apothecaries in the Middle Ages. Their erect, bushy growth, only three feet high, is better left unpruned except for removing dead wood and old flower heads.

My favourite rose, 'Celestial', is of ancient origin belonging to the Alba group which includes the taller, pre-sixteenth-century 'White Rose of York'. Celestial's grey-green foliage and soft pink, semi-double flowers has superb perfume; only prune where necessary. When I discovered Celestial in our Ayrshire garden, nobody seemed to know its true name; "It's one of the old Ayrshire roses," I was told.

My collection grew. Those gorgeous floriferous Damask roses whose strong taller bushes are clothed with glowing pink or deeper glowing pinks for a long season, their double, or semi-double flowers sometimes quartered, with incurving centres like 'La Ville de Bruxelles' who was produced by M. Vibert in France in 1849; or another Damask, 'Leda', the Painted Damask, which is only three feet high.

Each and every rose has a fascinating history; some were produced by enthusiasts, whereas the older species roses such as the enchanting Threepenny Bit Rose, were "found" by Reginald Farrer the great botanist and explorer in China in 1914. This rose makes an ornamental hedge or shrub, its fine fern-like leaves turning crimson and purple in autumn, amongst which a profusion of bright orange-red hips glow following small star-like, lilac-pink flowers. It is easier to take a pair of shears in order to trim back trailing shoots which are covered with minute thorns, when the "hedge" is ready for light pruning.

The Damask roses must be pruned very differently. Their initial stems must be allowed to grow to a reasonable height, varying from three to five feet; at the desired point, they should be pruned to encourage fresh growth. Each following season, many Damasks produce a wealth of strong young shoots after profuse and beautiful, fragrant flowering. Once again these are shortened, so far, and in varying heights so that flower buds can develop without crowding each other out within their leafy forest. Some new shoots will emerge from the roots, and unless the lower parts are congested, these shoots are better grown on as before. I learned about pruning this type of rose the hard way, having been taught to cut out occasional old branches from their base as one does with shrubs such as philadelphus. The result was a horrible forest of poor growth which grew worse the more it was cut. Now I realise that one must keep the main stems however thick they become, and then, one shortens back the eventual current year's growth, and of course any dead wood. It is a very simple operation and very time-consuming, but think of the glory these roses will bring to the following summer's wealth, when one's work and love is repaid a hundredfold.

There are other groups such as enchanting Moss roses, Musk roses, Climbing Noisettes, Briars and Burnet roses, these last being parents of such wonderful recent introductions as 'Fruhlingsgold' and 'Gold Wings'.

Perhaps you will now be encouraged to collect "old roses", suitable for your own garden, knowing that there are so many different shapes and sizes, each with wondrous fragrance of its own. For those readers who have already become enchanted with their beauty and variations, the advice on pruning may be of some assistance. What a wonderful Christmas present they would make, in which you and your friends will rejoice for many years to come.

FOR EDWARD, SIX YEARS OLD THIS DAY

I want to be an artist
When I grow up big and strong,
And paint the way I watch my Dad
Or draw, the whole day long.

I'll imitate those funny men,
Pink clouds that hurry by:
Hugh elephants with curling trunks,
Winged birds that sail the sky.

But not those busy bantam cocks
Or endless farms and rolling sea.
I'll bring alive the folk that dance
And sing with music swinging free.

But now I'm just a little boy,
Hop-scotching down a car-lined street.
I'm staring up at great big men,
My world's around their endless feet.

All Saints Day
November 1st 1988

'ON A COLD AND FROSTY MORNING'

June 1987

Do you watch the moon in its customary phases, in the manner of wise country folk of past days, before present advance satellite weather forecasts? I always watch the moon, and one late October night was entranced to see a complete, and very strange ring of light encircling, at a little distance, an almost full moon. It was a curious phenomenon and I wondered what this might foretell — a sudden dramatic change from unusually mild weeks at this late season?

Dahlias growing in sheltered corners were still blooming; even lobelia and pine-apple-scented geraniums remaining in urns, were untouched; there was still wonderful radiance and colour in the garden. Gentians were brilliant carpets of blue.

After a sharp frosty night suddenly all was gone; the following morning All Saints Day rejoiced, as brilliant daylight emerged out of bitter darkness.

One of the loveliest sights that morning were red-stemmed dogwoods growing in the Wild Garden. Seen from the Terrace walk, as sparkling sunshine warmed glow-ing stems, they are always one of the loveliest sights of a winter garden. *Cornus alba* 'Elegantissima', with variegated silvery white foliage, is ornamental all the year round, while the Wedding Cake species, *C. contraversa* 'Variegata', aptly described, its finer branches ascending in layers is unusually beautiful.

The maple family is a large one; those originating mainly from the Far East include particularly ornamental species more suited to the smaller garden. Many cul-tivars of the "Japanese" *Acer palmatum* species have been raised, which are at their best in well-drained soils sheltered from cold winds especially from the east.

One of my favourites is *A. P.* 'Senkaki', the Coral Bark Maple, an invaluable small tree, particularly for winter effect, its leaves turning soft canary yellow in autumn. Our tree has been protected each winter with fir branches or pea stakes, laid and tied over a wire netting cage which is removed only after the last frost of early June is safely away. Other, possibly delicate shrubs are protected in the same way until they are firmly established or too large to cover. It is well worth the effort of doing this in order to grow something beautiful and uncommon, bringing high-lights to the garden. Such treasures as violets can be grown around these shrubs, encouraging them to produce early unspoilt flowers beneath an added canopy.

My heart jumped for joy the other morning when I looked at a seedpan, covered with another for protection; there, at last were tiny cyclamen seedlings, germinating freely. They were *C. neapolitan*, sown in springtime and set on gravel in the shade of a holly bush. Except for removing an occasional weed they were left in peace; quite suddenly they were on the move. Many people say that seed is much the best way to grow cyclamen; dry corms are hard to bring into life; occasionally one can obtain plants "in the green". Last Christmas I was given a three-inch pot of cyclamen in a little basket; these were certainly of the wild *persicum* type bought in a big store in London. They flowered for a long time and died down. In the early summer after resting, they began to grow, so I took a chance, planting them in a special bed beside a young magnolia where they have since become a leafy cluster, now covered with leaves. I watch them with great expectations.

Another unexpected ploy is in attempting to root strands of clematis in gravelly corners. Fair-haired Saya loves flowers, and when she was seven years old was constantly picking bouquets — sometimes my treasures! — for Mummy or Granny. This time she brought a strand of the reliable old *Clematis* x *Jackmanii* which winds its way through *Cotoneaster horizontalis* and tropaeoleum, outside our kitchen window. We put the clematis in a vase in the cool sun-parlour, but next day it looked miserable. I could not bring myself to throw an old favourite away, and thought of half burying it in another sheltered path. It has never looked back, so time will tell if the experiment is successful.

Have you ordered any new rose bushes as yet? I am intrigued with a beautiful, old-time tea rose called 'Polly'', bred in 1927, and rediscovered by Andersons, the famous Deeside nursery near Aberdeen. 'Polly' is ivory suffused with yellow, melting into a warm creamy pink centre with a powerful fragrance, to me the quality which means most in a rose. Vigorous bushes make 'Polly' "a must" for both my gardens. Another reliable pale pink fully scented rose which looks equally beautiful called 'Blesma Soul', is named in honour of the British Limbless Ex-Servicemen's Association. Plants that have stories attached to their names are especially interesting to grow. Now is the time to get roses planted before really hard weather overtakes the countryside.

POPPIES

October 1989

Poppies! What do their childlike morning faces mean to us, at many seasons of the year, but especially now when Remembrance Sunday draws near? There are poppies of entirely different forms and varying species: they may bring us joy and happiness with memories of days we never want to forget, which we lock up safely in those precious jewel boxes of memory. There are poppies which wake up in springtime — those tough little Welsh or Icelandic poppies, their shining yellow faces appearing unexpectedly among rockery stones, or comfortably establishing their seedlings amongst herbaceous plants where perhaps they are not really welcome: or fixing their tough fleshy white roots firmly among those of spreading shrub roses where they instinctively know that they will be difficult to remove, each seedling capable of making a handsome, sun-catching plant. In our hearts we are glad to see them year by year, wherever they establish themselves, knowing that they are once again arising to knock on so many doors down memory lane.

Spring weather with its fickleness and fabrications of warm, vibrant days is long past, when the beauty of willow warblers' melodies filled woodlands around garden and river bank: their songs impel our hearts to rise in utter joy. It is at that time of year we notice those dead looking clusters of Himalayan poppies waking up, like hedgehogs, disturbed from among leafy refuge as morning sun penetrates and warms their cosy blankets. Pointed furry, ear-like leaves are arising from these awakening meconopsis; soft blue green; some species with reddish colouring on their undersides; in a short while each plant is clothed in beauteous greenery of widening foliage, and as April's days become the merry month of May, a wealth of blue cup-like saucers clothe strong stems with ethereal loveliness. Sunlight dancing on the rear of sky blue petals creates the appearance of translucence, and of wonderment.

It is upon these same flowers that my eyes become fixed each morning from our bedroom window. Cicely Crewdson's hybrid gazing up along sunlit grass to meet my own gaze of fantasy and dreamland. Further up, in front of old yellow azalea bushes, a large bed of George Sheriff's treasure, found during his travels in the Himalayas in 1938, their midnight blue petals and broader, softer leaves distinguishing them at a glance. *Meconopsis* 'Loch Inch' and *M.* 'Slieve Donard', each differing somewhat in form and colour, but to someone who loves these poppies, they are easily known at a glance as friends, waiting to greet myself and each other at breakfast time.

Divide these herbaceous poppies in the autumn and they will become busy, growing into further useful plants. If you undertake this operation in the spring they sometimes resent disturbance. Meantime, clothe them liberally with leafmould, compost or rotted farmyard manure; winter's rest is necessary to their well-being as it is to all creatures, great and small; snow is like champagne to poppies and to so many sleeping plants.

What about our little summer poppies, Shirley poppies and the like? Cheerful annuals, frequently self-sown, will waken with springtime. Later, when harvest fields are rich with golden corn, scarlet poppies are reborn; along railway banks where ground is dry and sunbaked, children delight in their brilliance. When Flanders fields were scarred and torn, these poppies returned to clothe that saddened countryside, and ever since those terrible days of trench warfare, these small wild flowers have remained symbolic of enduring hope in victory to bring peace and goodwill to all mankind.

We all have our thoughts, our prayers, our dreams; our hopes for our children's children, and their future safety. Our thankfulness to all those brave people who fought in many lands in the cause of freedom, and who never returned home. In these coming weeks when poppies are bravely worn, let us also not forget those at our firesides now, who were "out there" and came home safely.

November winds may blow, and snow may gently fall, providing safe cover for our many sorts of poppies — yellows, blues, pinks and scarlet reds; remember that they are only sleeping, waiting, re-invigorated, for spring's awakening lights. Swelling buds tumble off their harvest of brilliant leaves into autumn winds, predicting that new life will be born when the call of spring comes.

Gaze into the faces of these freedom loving flowers. Poppies can share our dreams, and show us that resurrection is not an idle fantasy.

TAPESTRY OF COLOUR

November 1984

It was already the second of November; yet another balmy day dawned in this extraordinarily beautiful frost-free autumn. Sunshine bathed the garden in even richer colours than usual, having had those extra weeks of warmth to mellow and mature every variety of plant life.

Leaves fell carefully to the ground from time to time; that wonderfully exciting sound of a sudden leaf drop, depleting a whole tree of her tresses in a single moment, was still but a filament in one's memory this unusual autumn, for there had been no frost to sever the cambium and cause this strange pitter patter on quiet cold mornings. Even maple leaves were hanging on to the last moment, resilient with glory of ruby reds and golden yellows.

Lovely sugar pink nerines glowed with happiness in sheltered corners; these South African bulbous flowers enjoy growing in well drained places where their bulbs can absorb all possible sunlight and warmth. Cape lilies — *Galtonia capensis* — continue to flower happily sheltered by azalea bushes; if comfortably settled they will soon form useful clumps producing creamy white bells which last for many weeks.

In front of these, a border of catmint which had been lightly clipped over a couple of months back in order to rid it of untidy flower stalks, was showing flowers once more among a sea of welcome grey-blue foliage, treated in the same way. Golden marjoram, continues to flower with abandon, not a weed showing through this thick golden carpet. To run one's hands through its foliage and then inhale the perfume is an unforgettable pleasure.

What worthwhile joy it is to have dahlias blooming in November their petals still of perfect formation particularly those elegant medium or small cactus varieties which bring exciting colours to any garden. Unless dahlias are being grown for show, they are much greater value and ornamentation to a garden of variation like our own when grown in little groups among other herbaceous plants, where each group can show itself off to advantage: even if some should become a little dilapidated this scarcely shows when their next door neighbours are easy-going Michaelmas daisies, bergamots and phloxes. One of the newer Michaelmas daisies, *Aster novae-angliae* 'Andenken an Alma Pötschke', is well worth growing, its colour quite startling — salmon-tinged bright rose flowers on branching heads — not one of those unwanted varieties which spread in all directions. A newer variety *A.* 'Firefly' was added because of the name — Firefly being my much loved grey pony: her mother, Gypsy, was my first Fell mare, from Heltondale, and her sire the grey thoroughbred Without Benefit, who travelled Cumberland for the Hunters Improvement Society about 1935, leaving many good foals in the district including my own, a much wanted birthday present when I was twelve years old.

The reliable old fashioned *A.* 'September Ruby' is equally good, with colourful terminal heads, excellent to cut for the house. A frill or base of long lasting mahonia, yew, or thuya arranged in a vase or bowl makes a wonderful base into which dahlias and these other faithful friends of autumn can be added, without too much trouble in creating a long lasting arrangement. Thuya holds the most delicious scent which always reminds me of *Stories from Arabian Nights*. Mother used to read these aloud to us as we sat round the fire on winter evenings after tea. We three usually sat on the floor, while Father sat in comfort reading his newspaper or *Farmer and Stockbreeder*.

Perhaps it was taking a risk to leave urns and tubs outside still filled with geraniums, *Helichrysum petiolare*, fuchsias and the like; they were blooming away happily, having put on tremendous growth. Boxes of cuttings, dibbled in some weeks since, will provide a wealth of plants next season, if one should be unlucky enough to lose their parents.

It was such a lovely afternoon, just right for planting tulips; a little sharp sand below each bulb will help them to form roots easily and to keep moisture draining freely. The evening sky became a dream-world of lavenders of all shades beyond tall beech and sycamore trees which shelter the garden from storms. Further west and north, lavenders changed to flame and gold. One simply had to stand and stare and fill one's whole being with the beauty of the evening; outlined trees against the heavens made the scene the more poignant.

Light was fading fast; tools were hung up in the potting shed; it was time to go indoors.

Quite unexpectedly overnight fickle winds changed to blow fiercely from the north while torrential rain fell unabated; at three o'clock in the afternoon on November the 3rd, snow fell with determination; the world had become white and bleak.

What must my treasures in the garden feel now, I wondered anxiously! At bedtime between two and three inches of snow lay solidly on the ground.

Morning came; winds had shifted round; disappearing snow lay unhappily in sudden flight; sunshine returned; strangely, dahlias, pansies and even unseasonable auriculas were flowering unharmed as if nothing untoward had ever taken place. The vagaries of our capricious British climate . . .

LOOK UP!

Look up! Look up into the morning sky:
Those fleecy clouds bespeak the coming day;
As drifts of newborn lambs with snowy ewes
They drift and pass into a realm of fantasy.
For in their place those sparkling lights of dawn,
Those blinding shafts that dazzle, and defray
Glad gleams of newborn light, that precious thing,
That priceless thing that gladdens and displays
The God given gift of dawn,
The break of day reborn.

Look up! Look up into the midnight sky
And see the stars, the wealth of Heaven unfurled
Galaxies of crowned celestial glory
Watching in majesty around our tiny world,
While summer's early dawn, transparent mists
Steal countryside's awakening happiness.
With warmth and colours richly laid upon the scene
Where butterflies and drowsy bees the flowers caress,
Since birds sing summer evensongs of praise
We too with joy our earthbound hearts must raise.

Look up! Look up into autumn's sky
The flowing warmth, on still November days
When sunlight puzzles through the resting trees
And all things rest in their mysterious ways.
Apples, radiant upon the upmost bough
Lingering long to tell the tale of spring;
Proud blackbirds hearten us below, with songs of joy
In frost filled dawns what joyousness they bring.
Long grass lies bended, hoar-spangled, pearly
Evenings draw in fast, stars twinkle early.

Look up! Look up to chill winter's sky
And read the certain tale of heaven retold
Be there fierce fright'ning storms or long, low light,
See the wise plan as withered months unfold
Though days and nights equivalent may be
Red berries glow, becoming food and cheer;
Glad Christmas weeks bestir brown squirrels' stores,
Warm, leafstrewn woods close fast their forest doors,
Where all things rest, and wait, for spring is near,
But if your head be wary, breathe the wind
For in its strength the power to heal, you'll find.

1990

128

STARS OF THE MORNING

December 1988

"Stir up", the theme of prayers for the last Sunday in November, also reminds gardeners that we cannot lie in idleness through wintery weeks, when frost outside makes it much more conducive to read a book by the fire, or to be stirring our Christmas puddings so that they can mature before the feast day arrives.

Wild winds of late November easily damaged wall roses, forgotten because there were other things, perhaps more pressing, which claimed our attention; but those precious long new growths which will form basic branches two years hence may be torn or bent irreparably. These should be tied, possibly in arched shape, their tips removed, thus forcing flower buds to form along the length of their branches. If rotted farmyard manure is available, spread some not only close to the stem, but further out, to encourage feeding roots to become busy.

Young trees or bushes must be checked at intervals for their stakes may have loosened; lately I found a cherry toppled over, supported only with a garden cane, but within a tubular tree guard. These guards are usually excellent, keeping both wind and rabbits at bay, encouraging sapling trees to put on growth in order to reach the sunlight. But lately — oh horrors! — when Alistair, our forester, looked round his young trees and came to a small plantation of oaks growing on a somewhat stony bank created in order to make a car park, the guards were creating homes for families of field mice within their protective covering. These oaks had grown so well, and were suddenly nibbled to death. The stony bank and the guards were making ideal winter quarters for the mouse world.

That extraordinary circle round November's moon certainly brought a rapid change in our weather pattern. Little Saya and I were out with the ponies on an exceptionally mild Sunday afternoon. Saya always rode her lovely grey Welsh cross thoroughbred Tara who came to us as a very green three-year-old; I rode darling old Heather, a pet black Fell mare now twenty-five years old who, besides going at a spanking trot in harness, had produced some of our best foals. She was so safe to ride with the grandchildren.

"Look, Granny," Saya called excitedly, "Look! it's really snowing." Later that evening my little dogs were jumping through deep snow. How wonderful for the plant world it is to see them blanketed safely, before hard frost takes over; it is like a little miracle that they are able to adapt themselves without harm from entirely opposite conditions and frequently in reverse, all too quickly. In spite of a real wintery week, there are daisies and buttercups blooming on our lawn — children's flowers for the children's festival, in this season of Advent.

Most border flowers have been cut down. Already young growths are making their way to form next season's flowering stems; it always seems inspiring to be aware that nothing ever dies, but in some form, which we do not fully understand, everything in the whole of Creation will find rebirth.

Herbaceous plants multiply readily and now is the time to divide old clumps, discarding some so that there is room in our borders for the addition of something new, to give more colour where needed and to bring added excitement. I feel quite sad having to cast out good plants which were unusual when purchased. That marvellous sedum, 'Autumn Joy', still full of ruby colour despite frost and snow, must be divided and replanted and half its numbers given away or left to fend for itself in grassy corners. Likewise, *Ligularia przewalskii*, its ornamental black spires covered with chrome yellow butterfly-type flowers. I bought this at the Chelsea Flower Show in the early fifties chiefly because it was grown by a Polish nurseryman and I understand, named after a Polish race horse. We owe such a debt to the Polish people who stood up to the forces of evil even with their horses against tanks, at the beginning of the horrors of 1939; some of the Polish officers spent their leaves with us at Dalemain throughout the war. I well remember some of the older men, who became our friends, talking sadly to my father of all they had left behind. One had a factory on his estate where perfumes were made from plants that grew on one of his farms.

My new ornamental *L. przewalskii*, still growing in our two gardens forty years later, produces many good offspring, some of which require to be moved to other sites, but they are each splendid individual plants. The flower spikes are most useful to use in floral decorations in the house. A mixed vase in the Chinese Drawing Room suits their blooms which blend with the colour and patterns on the eighteenth century wallpaper.

When gaps are created, fork, weed and manure in readiness for something new. What about variegated figwort which is still clothed with cream and green young growth; this is an excellent plant. Or *Symphytum peregrinum* 'Variegatum' which has startlingly bright leaves and purple-pink flowers. It is a striking plant which will grow in sun or partial shade. I am planting the white *Heuchera* Green Ivory in the front of my border.

After the garden becomes more orderly and forked or dug where necessary, give it a good coating of farm manure, old rotted compost or leafmould, and leave for the weather to do its silent work.

Meanwhile we can enjoy lattice-like beauty of leafless branches, each tree or shrub recognisable by lace-like quality, every one entirely different in form and pattern to its neighbour. Watching morning sunlight stream through frosted, snow-laden branches makes one rejoice, gazing into a sparkling picture that ever remains in one's mind.

No sooner had the snow vanished, nourishing soil and plants as it disappeared, than exciting flowers of the winter season put forth a few precious blooms.

Some years ago after the Grove had been felled and replanted with a very few important trees to shelter flowering shrubs, we planted a standard cherry. Growing in the most favoured situation, protected by old hollies and old-fashioned white lilacs, this tree, now about fifteen feet high with a wide canopy, may be the frost hardy, bell-flowered, Taiwan cherry, *Prunus campanulata*. Rosy-red flowers produced from very early to mid spring, hang with amazing grace; I can even look upon topmost blooms from our bedroom window. Each winter I watch for these unusually early flowers, or stand near its attractive trunk, gazing up into a jigsaw of elegant, twiggy branches outlined against clear, hurrying skies, and marvel at so much beauty.

Winter jasmine never fails to bloom, clothing walls with elegant sprays of star-like jewels of gold, proclaiming the season of Advent: they really are like stars of the morning. Nearby a few hellebores are pushing up snowy faces, each plant in its own way singing its carol for Christmas.

WISHES

While Carols rang clear for the Babe of us all,
How many wishes winged up to the skies;
Those wishes and prayers are fulfilled, and o'er spilled
In these two precious babies; Oh what a surprise!

Our wishes winged swift on the cold frosty air
For *one* blue-eyed babe, who'd bring joy to us three.
Bright stars and clear candles they twinkled and shone
While we danced and we sang round the fair Christmas tree.

Then, *two* little babies winged into our home
From somewhere out there, — from a land yet unknown.
Two little babies need two little beds
For to cradle them softly; lay down their sweet heads.

Twice ten tiny fingers
Twice ten tiny toes,
Two strong wakeful voices
And tiny snub nose.

Now, we've two real, live babies,
Winged safe from the skies,
While joy bells ring clear
For their bright sparkling eyes.

Lovely soft faces like apples that glow
In our garden at harvest, the best that we know.
Fingers that hold tight to say "we are here"
We are those wishes from out over there.

*Written for Jane, Robert and Hermione when the twins were born on
October 2nd 1990.*

November 1990

FROM THE FOREST'S FERNY FLOOR

January 1991

December: clear cold night skies filled with stars, full of wonderment, as one stands and gazes into the deep, dome of Heaven and the Great Beyond. Which was the star which hung over the stable at Bethlehem? Snow clouds, drifting nearer: what will this night foretell? The mysteries of Christmas drawing nearer day by day.

Plant life stabilised to meet the certain onslaught of winter. We must do our best to protect and shelter these amazing forms of life, before thankfully going indoors to the family and the fireside.

Our North Country gardens are not usually like those of the warmer parts of our islands. We expect winter's approach and wrap up somewhat tender shrubs with bracken or fir branches; half-hardies are moved to protective quarters in good time, unless we are caught napping. Over and over one answers or listens to the same old question, "How hardy is this plant, or shrub?" "Will it stand up to *our* weather?"

It is quite right to enquire, for we in the north welcome and expect a proper winter so that buds may lie dormant and rest. The long, warm autumn produced a flush of unwanted growth which should have been preserved for spring; in addition, autumn's tremendous harvest will be a burden on fruiting qualities the following season. Some trees, such as beech, are frequently biennial bearers, and certain apple trees also have the same habit.

Never mind these vagaries of nature. Amongst the wealth of beech masts, forming crunchy-brown, colourful carpets amid leaflike mosses, describing Persian designs, I'm already watching for golden buds of aconites, sure harbingers of spring. Among these nests of nuts, early flowers find natural shelter, which is the most important thing we can give our plants.

Lately I was shown a middle-aged friend's garden extending round a somewhat windswept farmhouse which he said was being "landscaped and planted". "What would I do?" our host enquired of me. "Plant hedges," was my immediate answer, instead of gazing upon the few forlorn shrubs planted of late and a dreary bed of heathers and gentians.

There were already magnificent old lime trees beyond the lawn fence, whose stature "landscaped" and enhanced the garden, but hedges would give protective cosiness. Cotoneaster grow quite quickly and could shelter more permanent yew, beech or common hornbeam, *Carpinus betulus*: the latter creates a beautiful hedge. Where archways are required as entrances to a further lawn or garden, some plants can be left to grow, twining their topmost branches into an arch while supple enough to bend.

When Constance Spry, that famous gardener of recent years, made her garden on the windswept island of Gigha off the Mull of Kintyre, she erected a double fence of rabbit netting round special areas of the garden, leaving a space of about eight inches between the rolls of netting. The winds hit the outer fence, divesting its force, so that the inner fence played havoc with the gale. Wonderful plants were grown in this west coast garden so long as they were thus protected.

If that farm garden were mine, double netted fences would be erected forthwith to give hedges and shrubs a good start. Since there was plenty of room in the field beyond, a shelter belt on the windward side would give an atmosphere of warmth; Norway spruce interplanted with hardwoods would be suitable, the former being gradually cut out for Christmas trees. If rabbits were around, spiny Sitka spruce would repel them while hardwoods could be protected with easily erected tube guards.

Sitkas form the most beautiful downward hanging cones, usually found at the crown of tall trees. Some such trees fell in our Huntfield woods last winter, but, in spite of lying in saddened disarray on the woodland floor the hot summer ripened seed buds and still produced a wealth of cones.

When the time came for the christening of our grandchildren, the twin babies in December, we cut the small topmost branches from these Sitkas to take part in the decorations at Dalemain. One leader, covered with magnificent, long, downward hanging cones was set into a big log, becoming a very special Christmas tree, displayed on an old chopping table in the big kitchen. It looked magnificent, while others, supported by sheep netting in large brass containers, decorated the hall and drawing room, together with variegated ivies, holly, yew and boxwood: a supply of water at their base, for they need to drink as well as flowers. Streamers of yew, holly, cones and such like, attached to ropes, decorated staircases and the Old Hall where celebration parties took place.

Amidst this wealth of woodland beauty and its harvest of splendour decorating both our home and Dacre's candlelit church, these two precious babies were baptised: George, whose name means a husbandman or farmer, while Beatrice, with her small smiling face, means a friend. Let us hope and pray that they will grow up to love and protect this beautiful countryside. Each generation plants and sows for the future. We have tried to dig richly and to sow with care; we must continue to look upwards, towards the dawn, entrusting our labours into strong, young hands, which we hope will carry on our work.

CAROLS IN THE CHRISTMAS GARDEN

December 1985

December is never a dull time in the garden. Consider the countryside, the beauty of leaves that have never left their parent trees — silver birch, hazel and many more, catching every gleam of sunlight, particularly dramatic at this season, lighting up grasses by the waterside in a startling manner. Somehow one never forgets these moments, more precious than the fullness of a summer's scene.

Berries give great pleasure, their polished surface glowing even on the dullest day — until so many of them are polished off by hungry birds as if they were revelling in their favourite plum puddings. Migrating redwings and fieldfares chortle with delight, well hidden by branches, while they have feasted, before moving on to the safety of tall beech trees for yet another meal. Our best and most colourful firethorns are cleared frequently; even so, they are worth growing and if planted round corners of house walls, many escape the attention of winged diners.

I have a very difficult little garden to clothe which came into being as a "secret" garden after the Georgian front of my home was built across the front of the earlier E-shaped Elizabethan house. Known as the "Kitchen Court" in 18th-century accounts, it only gets real sunshine in summertime, while high winds funnel down over roof-tops, making the atmosphere feel cold: but somehow, being "within the house", frost seldom worries plants during autumn or late spring at least, when it may ruin blossoming trees elsewhere. It is here, on an almost sunless wall, that pyracantha berries make glorious, long lasting displays. *P.* 'Orange Glow' is frost hardy; clusters of small, five-petalled white flowers decorate its spiny evergreen branches in summertime. So this difficult little courtyard garden has an occasional advantage.

Cotoneasters, too, make wonderful spectacles, their clusters of brilliant berries hanging invitingly on tall hybrids such as *C.* x *watereri* 'Cornubia', which bears scarlet fruit in profusion. Its near relation, *C.* x *W.* 'Exburiensis' produces yellow berries seldom touched by birds and is well worth growing, becoming an ornamental figurehead in the winter garden.

Jasmine is well known with its starry yellow showers of flowers, so long as its long growths are pruned hard after flowering: don't forget to do this in order to allow time for early flowering buds to form. What about sweet scented witch hazels, one of my favourite shrubs. *Hamamelis mollis*, the original Chinese species, is more fragrant than any of the more showy hybrids and will grow to fifteen feet in a mild district, but considerably less in our area. *H.* x *intermedia* 'Pallida', 'Westerstede' and 'Diane' all have beautiful yellow or orange flowers; they like good rich, loamy soil, not liable to dry out, and need virtually no pruning. They enjoy leafmould and sphagnum moss peat, and do not like limy conditions.

I was transfixed with the beauty of a very graceful shrub whose golden leaves appeared like those of a particularly finely wrought elm, catching every gleam of wintery sunlight as they are slow to fall to the ground. Each somewhat pointed, oval leaf shows the network of its veined system, like needlework, the whole framework spreading as a golden table cloth above a bed of sleeping candelabra primulas. This

Neillia sinensis is well worth growing in soil that does not readily dry out. In early summer little semi-pendant trails of rosy-pink flowers are an added beauty.

Nandina domestica 'Firepower' is a more unusual flamboyant shrub to grow. A select form of the Sacred Chinese Bamboo, its leaves remain through most winters, in brilliant shades of cream, orange and red. It is said to be an easy customer, but for safety it is remaining in a pot in our cold greenhouse for its first northern winter.

It is quite amazing the different forms of holly that can be grown — the more usual *Ilex* x *altaclerensis* 'Golden King' and variations of *I. aquifolium* 'Silver Queen' are really colourful, but there are plenty other varieties for those who seek. A particularly attractive clone grows on either side of a large stone pineapple at Huntfield on the edge of open woodland, for hollies really are woodlanders and need shelter to give of their best. They need protecting from rabbits, but whether they have berries or not, their foliage brightens the dullest day in winter.

Green hollies make splendid shelter for less hardy neighbours, such as magnolias; they also make wonderfully warm hedges. Every plant or shrub needs a "nurse plant" to help it along, and few, except parkland trees, like to grow in isolation. Whatever you think of planting this season will repay a hundred-fold if you really provide for their comfort and prosperity.

Already winter flowering cherries are ablaze with glory. *Prunus subhirtella,* 'Autumnalis Rosea' is in full glory in many gardens, its semi-double, blush pink blossoms almost fragile in appearance. In my gardens leaves of meadow saffron, the so-called Autumn Crocus, are already showing beneath these cherries' spreading branches. In a very short time *Prunus dulcis* 'Macrocarpa', the rich pink almond, will be decorating the countryside; it is particularly sensational when growing in the edge of sheltering wood-lands.

The best flowering shrub, for the bleaker weeks of winter, is *Viburnum fragrans,* whose praises I never fail to extol to anyone who asks "What is the best shrub to plant?" Its sweet-scented blossoms are a constant joy, and are in flower from early October for almost half the year — what more can one ask? The old species *V. fragrans* is more scented than its richer pink variety, *V.* x *bodnantene.* A few sprays can easily be spared to make a posy tied with late blooming roses and carried to the baby's crib for Christmas Day: then with joyful hearts we can truly sing the beautiful traditional carol, "Whence is that goodly fragrance flowing, stealing our senses all away." With praise and thankfulness we can feel that the glory of *our* gardens has contributed to the joy of Christmas.

FAMILY HOLIDAY

(Especially for Hermione Aged Four)

They'd never been to London
Three hundred miles away;
Friend William in his cosy home,
Invited them to stay.

He drove them in his motor car
Historic sights to see,
And when they'd been around them all
He brought them home for tea.

The Guards upon their horses
In splendour, sheer delight.
Hermione stood beside them —
A truly marvellous sight.

The Tower, the Queen's own Palace,
A bus she liked the most;
Or magic staircase up or down
With her untiring host.

"What would you like for luncheon?'
  From off the menu wide;
"I'd really like some custard,
  And a sausage, nicely fried.

"Waving from her Palace
  The Queen of certain knew
  It was Hermione waving back
  While she was passing through.

"I want to be a black lady!"
  There were plenty everywhere.
  Of all the sights she went to see
  She'd simply watch and stare.

To the babies in their carry cots
It never meant a thing,
But — they all went off to London
To have a little fling.

March 1991

GOLDEN GLORIES BRING CHRISTMAS CHEER

December 1985

All is not gold that glisters, but golden colours in our gardens and woodlands at this season of the year are truly glamorous and heart-warming, especially when winter sunshine glows with abundance on these treasures planted long since, with thought and care. In sheltered corners where arrowlike sunbeams glance with delight on variegated shrubs and climbers, all past efforts to give them "a good start" are well rewarded.

This is the season to plant more of these golden leafed beauties which can enliven any garden in winter time, but since so many shrubs arrive in containers they can be planted carefully when the weather is open and ground free of frost. Should conditions be unsuitable, trees can be stood in sheltered positions or better still, heeled into the earth and protected with branches to keep Jack Frost at arm's length.

Ivies are among the most rewarding glamorous beauties to plant, and none more colourful than *Hedera colchica* 'Dentata Variegata', whose large, parti-coloured, pointed leaves readily cover walls, giving added joys of providing roosting places for little birds when dusk falls, or when bitter snowdriven storms make living out of doors a nightmare. I planted this ivy beside a doorway into the garden, where it could scramble up a west-facing wall and cover the entire stone entrance, giving the feeling of entering "a secret garden." Another smaller leaved ivy, *H. helix* 'Gold Heart', is a perfect wall-coverer with tiny gilded pointed leaves. Either can be easily propagated from small twiggy pieces, popped into the ground at the foot of a new site, assisted by a handful of sharp sand or gravel which encourages new root systems to develop.

Shrub roses of some of the old species types, or of *rugosa* varieties, frequently hold on to their highly ornamental leaves for a very long time. One of the latter is 'Roseraie de l'Hay' which makes quite a handsome bush, and like many of this group is more or less perpetual flowering; its wine-purple flowers flaunt their richness with glorious scent, while corn coloured leaves remain glorious deep into winter; the additional benefit of growing *rugos*a roses is their enormous, ornamental hips.

The type *Rosa rugosa* grows wild in China and the Far East. They are most useful shrubs to grow in poor soil and difficult conditions, making superb hedges where there is sufficient space for them to develop and display their beauty.

A completely different, and much smaller shrub, is *Spiraea Japonica*, 'Gold Flame', which has been grown successfully in both our gardens, although it is a relatively new variety. Young spring growth is startling gold turning softer yellow as the season progresses. It is a useful shrub for a rock garden, lending colour and providing shelter for small bulbs; or to grow beside water where its reflections can dazzle a pool.

Thinking of good situations for small bulbs and corms, berberis of many varieties and sizes give superb shelter to treasures such as baby cyclamen which flower late, just as the days become colder. A little group of *Cyclamen neapolitanum* flower without fail, tucked well out of frost beneath a low growing *Berberis stenophylla* 'Corallina

The Knot Garden, Dalemain

Rhododendron 'Spring Magic', Huntfield

Geese over Huntfield

Dacre Beck

Compacta', whose dark green leaves and clusters of rich orange flowers bloom in profusion in May and again in autumn. The choice *Berberis thunbergii* 'Aurea' has bright golden yellow foliage and is well worth growing, but needs more careful siting out of the way of cold winds and late frosts. It is fun to "have a go" at things more exotic, even though one has to take more trouble till they become established.

For many years we have erected winter shelters of branches tied to wigwams of stakes in order to protect shrubs or trees that are difficult to establish. When spring comes round again one can rejoice in the effort made to see such things as colourful Japanese maples pushing out elegant young leaves which will soon clothe their parents with glory and which might have been frosted if left unprotected through winter. Leave the cage and branches in place until frosts are past.

Dogwoods are easy subjects, and as with all the more common plants, new varieties are continually being produced. True plantsmen will walk round what appears to be a perfectly ordinary garden with hawklike eyes, ready to spot a "sport" or freak among the vegetation. Thus the choice *Cornus alba* 'Aurea' came into being, and when grown in an open sunny situation its soft golden leaves are a perfect foil against other contrasting colours. A much newer find by Alan Bloom is *Cornus sanguinea* 'Winter Flame'. The stems of this dogwood become an outstandingly brilliant flame in winter, its leaves gradually turning orange and yellow also as autumn wears on into winter. It shows off to best advantage in full sunlight.

Holly trees are rewardingly glamorous, especially when loaded with clusters of bright red berries in December. Their berries seem to be really plentiful this autumn, but it is the golden-leaved hollies that bring Christmas cheer when planted on the edge of woodlands or in sheltered sunlit positions. *Ilex* x *altaclerensis* 'Golden King' — female despite its name — has almost spineless leaves, and is a universal favourite, but there are many other varieties which bring interest and colour particularly during winter, with different shaped coloured leaves. *Ilex crenata* 'Golden Gem' is a dwarf, small-leaved holly of great merit, forming a flat-topped bush, bright golden in the dreariest months. An old-fashioned brilliant golden holly grows beside my grandparents' home in Perthshire. For sentimental reasons, and because the house and gardens are now a glory of past years when we were young, I have attempted to strike cuttings. Perhaps they will be lucky and form rootlets next spring, which will bring endless joy in future years, reminding me of happy days with much-loved grandparents and of the enormous old holly that shone with grandeur at all seasons of the year. Perhaps some of their berries will germinate also, for where they grew on the parent tree were other splendid varieties which hopefully will have fertilised these seeds.

A charming little holly known as the Hedgehog Holly, *Ilex aquifolium* 'Ferox Argentea', is well worth growing; its spiny leaves are cream-margined and though it will grow into a sizable shrub, it is very slow growing. I carried this little treasure home from the Harrogate Flower Show, and planted it in a favourable position in the Walled garden, but in days to come when it has grown somewhat it will be moved to a sunny little border on the edge of the Grove, which needs to be cheered up with variegated hollies, of which so many are available in present times.

The choice of golden-leaved plants and shrubs is endless; rowans, golden leyland cypresses, maples, cytisus, philadelphus, potentillas, besides many dwarf slow-growing conifers suitable for rockeries, stone troughs, or simply to plant along gravelled edges of borders where early crocus can accept their ready shelter. Dwarf junipers are among the loveliest and most useful; that delightful *Juniperus media* 'Old Gold' has grown in a round stone quern near our front door for many years, and has never ceased to lighten the darkness of winter. *Juniperus communis* 'Golden Showers', is another; its yellow-bronze winter colouring is later transformed into bright golden yellow. As it will eventually grow to about 20 cms, I planted one at the end of a short avenue of *Prunus pissardii* in the Grove, as a focal point, leading the eye towards a beautiful carriage archway. The archway was filled in, with stone similar to others used to build the high courtyard wall. Now the arch is draped with wisteria and *Clematis montana*, both climbers beginning to make a lovely show, quite unexpected in the little wood, the long lilac racemes of the wisteria catching every gleam of sunshine.

Do plant something golden to bring glory to your winter garden. Perhaps a kind friend will ask, "What would you like this Christmas?" They would readily guess what my choice would be.

PLEASURABLE CHRISTMAS PRESENTS

January 1989

Many of us have been given a plant for a Christmas present, and what welcome presents these make: azaleas covered with colourful buds and flowers, or cyclamen whose delicate petals remind us of pixies wearing cheery pointed caps as in some of our favourite fairy tales and in the world of fantasy and make-believe.

How are we to keep these plants in healthy condition, so that they may bring renewed joy another season? Remember they have lately been in a warm forcing atmosphere; even standing about in a draughty shop has been a shock. Azaleas have probably been lately potted into a peaty compost with little fertilizer and in pots that are not really big enough for root development, but making handy sizes for presents. My first reaction is to stand them in a bowl of water for an hour or two, spraying their leaves and flowers, even using a clean milk bottle for handiness. When time allows they are repotted into something larger depending on root systems. I am lucky having a ready source of rich acid soil and rotted leaf mould, and with coarse sand to aerate the mixture and a touch of bone meal, azaleas immediately look happier and can withstand dry conditions in the house. In a little while, towards the end of January, they will be watered, using phostogen, an easy and complete feed, and again throughout coming months at perhaps monthly intervals, to help them, like our hardy outdoor azaleas, to put on new growth and make fresh abundance of flower buds. Probably their second season will be poor in flowers, but it is much more important to encourage new growth.

Cyclamen are more difficult. Growers have amazing modern methods of raising seedlings enabling these to come to the prolific flowering size we see at Christmas. It is exciting if we manage to flower these corms again. Cyclamen grow in dry, stony conditions in the wild; their native homes are Turkey, Cyprus and further east, so we must never allow them to become waterlogged, though, like azaleas in household conditions, they need water and spray about every five days when blooming. Keep them in worthwhile condition even after the last flowers are dead and even if no longer growing in your sitting room: they will enjoy cooler conditions. I have a gardening friend who removes all her pot plants to a really cool dining room every night, and they love it!

My miniature cyclamen are standing happily on our bathroom window sill and on my dressing table close to a window which is open every night, and they have already flowered for two months. They are all sprayed and watered regularly and already have had a feed of phostogen to supply the nourishment they need after all the energy used in flowering continuously. Today most of my potted plants are standing out of doors on the gravel on this mild misty day — one must not forget to bring them in at dusk, although our grandchildren on holiday claim undivided attention! Do encourage children to help to look after your plants, and later they will want to grow their own "just like Granny showed us what ought to be done!"

When all fear of frost is past, stand these Christmas presents out of doors in a cool site, but bring them into the greenhouse or beside a window when autumn comes, top dress with riddled leafmould and sharp sand; rotted pine needles are even better for acid loving plants.

When tulips and hyacinths are grown in bowls, a few twiggy branches will support increasingly leggy flowers considerably more attractively than if they were tied with thin stakes and twine. Moss and little ferns will decorate earth or fibre and later should be heeled in, outside. In this way our pots and bowls can be made to look more natural.

Tokens to spend at garden centres conjure up a whole host of possibilities — what about planting one of those beautiful coloured ivies in a draughty or difficult situation? Even in midwinter ivies are always dressed to perfection. My favourite is the elegant small- to medium-leaved *Hedera helix* 'Goldheart': its rich green foliage with eye-catching golden yellow centres will grow successfully in shade or sun; somewhat slow until it can attach itself to stone or brick and then a fast grower, happily covering unsightly downspouts. *H. colchica* 'Paddy's Pride', somewhat larger leaved, again boasts central splashes of yellow. It is an ivy that will withstand hot sun or wild winter weather climbing up the high wall behind the herbaceous border along the Terrace at Dalemain — this wall, whose perfect stonework with its graceful cornice was built, or rebuilt, by Mr James Swingler for Sir Edward Hasell in 1685.

A slender, small-leaved ivy, *H. helix* ' Silver Queen', silver-grey with a white margin, is slow growing and never rampant, suitable for a small space. All ivies respond to clipping in order to keep them within bounds. My present venture is planting a pair of clematis, using the ivy as a "nurse" plant; their fragile stems can find refuge even in a gale when they climb, bringing further colour behind and above herbaceous plants. Remembering that ivy dries the soil, these clematis are planted eighteen inches out from the wall one on either side of their host, each set within a drain tile which is pushed firmly into the soil, on end, as protection against slugs. My choice was the lilac-violet-blue *Clematis* 'Perle d'Azur' to contrast delicately with the yellow of *H. colduca* 'Paddy's Pride'.

Clematis are available in so many varieties that in choosing an early flowering *montana* or later, larger flowering hybrids, one can have unbounded pleasure from their beautiful, long season of bloom.

The aftermath of Christmas presents will never cease to bring many of us untold joy; but don't put tokens away in a drawer as I sometimes do, in order to "keep them safe" and forget that they need to be used.

THE FOUR SEASONS

When winter steals across the land
And gardens rest in slumbers deep,
I hear the clearest peel of bells
That wakes the dreamers from their sleep —
Those purest drifts of living snow
Ring in life's daysprings whilst they grow.

The charming cherry gently sways
Those magic blossoms, calling spring,
Her branches laid with fairest flowers
Form choir stalls where birds watch and sing.
Apple blossom joins the swell
Of lilacs in the spring, they tell.

Where lilies hold their chaliced heads
With fragrance filled, in off'ring sweet.
White roses shadow on the lawn
Perfuming the air of noonday's heat.
The stable clock in steady rhyme
Calls, drowsily, in summertime.

Those sunkissed harvest days soon pass
Whose drowsy bees in foxglove bells
Murmur sweet nothings to the flowers;
While swallows sing their sad farewells,
Autumn's dance, flames woods with fire,
Robes flowers and field in rich attire.

December's fields are worked and ploughed
Her plants lie dormant, resting, bare;
Red robin wakes with mournful trill;
A mouse peeps up to blink and stare;
But in her gown of pure repose
Shines forth the wakeful Christmas rose.

February 1989

MIDWINTER'S MAGIC

December 1987

Winter is full of beauty; it is not a dead season in gardens and countryside, although it is the antithesis of summer's abundance with wondrously contrasting lights and shadows — the ethereal beauty of bare-leafed trees and lace-like texture of beech trees outlined against rosy skies at dawn.

Most important, it is the season of rest. It is not only we human beings who need sleep; equally, plant life must rest, or wear out with constant flowering, which happens to rose bushes in hot climates. Snow does untold good, especially when protecting plant life from bitter winds and frost. So when snow falls fast and deep, one can at least be thankful for its lasting benefit in our gardens.

This is when staking firmly is essential. Rubber-buckled tree ties, available from garden centres, are much the best to use, for they can be rebuckled as trees grow and do not cut into bark as those forgotten ties of binder twine. When this occurs, one can only cut the branches free and completely retie. It is not too late to continue pruning fruit trees and shrubs. Apples, gooseberries, red currants and many more should be cut back to three or so buds on *last* season's growth, unless fresh extended branches are required; where pruning is not carried out, so much growing energy is wasted as it is chiefly the last few inches of the tips which will bear fruit and this will be of much poorer quality if left unpruned.

Winter spraying of fruit trees is an important operation, using tar oil winter wash to kill grubs and moulds of various sorts which later awake to blemish fruit crops. Pick a quiet day for this task, when trees are dry and mild weather has returned.

Signs of an early spring seem foretold by the world of nature, or is it the mild prolonged season of autumn that has upset the calendar for rooks who were busy building around Hutton-in-the-Forest and Aikton early in December when we drove to Aikton Church some twenty miles north-west of Dalemain. The small Norman church is one of the most charming I know: it was here that Grandfather spent thirty-nine years as rector of this scattered agricultural parish where oak trees grow prolifically, the Celtic name, Aikton meaning the hamlet of oaks. After these contented years he inherited the responsibilities of Dalemain on the death of his older brother, John, squire for as many seasons.

We drove to plant two home-grown oaks in the churchyard as a memorial to Grandfather, followed by a short service of thanksgiving. The oaks must have benefited from the blessing, as they are both doing well!

Bulbs of many sorts have been pushing steadily upwards, and already cheerful aconites cause delight when their golden faces reflect wintery sunlight from sheltered corners.

Chinese witch hazels are well worth space in the smallest garden. The incomparable *Hamamelis mollis* is notable for sweetly scented, spider-like flowers clustering against bare twigs in winter, whilst hybrid witch hazels vary from coppery-red to bronze, some with leaves which colour fiery tints in autumn. It requires planting in sheltered corners.

The largest and most beautiful *H. mollis* known to me grows in my cousin's garden, near Lanrick, where we spent so many happy days when our grandparents were alive. They had recently bought a house beside the Bridge of Teith, and unknowingly, almost had the witch hazel cut down. Fortunately, he recognised this wintery-looking shrub in time; its life was spared, and being a keen gardener he is now so grateful that the axe remained in the tool shed. At this season, holly comes to mind. The variegated silvery margined variety is one of the most attractive, lighting up dark corners and growing reasonably fast; but remember, hollies are fundamentally woodland trees, and so require shelter, or better still, woodland conditions where sunshine can penetrate, to give of their best. Trimming longest branches, as with golden yew and many other shrubs grown for ornamentation, improves their colour and interest as a whole. I use these species for vases in the house, and being evergreen, they last well in water, so long as one takes off the lower leaves.

As early darkness falls we close up greenhouses and frames securely while brilliant frosty moonlight lights the countryside causing strange shadows to make us fall into reverie and gaze up into starlit heavens. We pause in heartfelt gratitude for Christmas and all it has meant throughout the centuries, realising how little we understand of the Creation; so much we take on trust; yet as we close the garden door at the end of another year we are assured that all our work, and all for which we have striven, will be rewarded by the certain coming of yet another spring — the rebirth of the countryside. Our hearts warm with gratitude and we give thanks to the Maker of all things.

MARY MOUSE'S CHRISTMAS TREAT

"Will you come to my party," Mrs Mouse said,
"Fancy asking us children to tea!"
"We'll have tea in my old fashioned kitchen
  And dance round an old Christmas tree."

The children came far to her party
In spite of blind blizzarding snow,
Hedges and treetrunks quite hidden,
They scarcely knew how they might go.

They met in the loveliest kitchen,
Oak cupboards and china displayed;
And a tree with long magical fircones,
Red crackers and candles arrayed.

But where's Mrs Mouse with her welcome?
She's gone to her cousin's abode;
She's gone off to visit the Town Mouse
Now she's deep in a drift on the road.

Just in case, so she thought, this might happen,
Mary Mouse left Dalemain with good care
Her house was alight with a welcome
And her presents laid under the stair.

So we danced and we sang in the firelight,
We crocodiled all round the house;
Ate sausages under the candles
Still waiting for dear Mrs Mouse.

On the fellside her carriage was stranded
The horse could pull it no more.
She wrapped up inside her fur jacket — sighed —
"I'll never leave home any more."

Saturday December 8th 1990

146

CHRISTMAS CHILDHOOD RELIVED

November 1986

Christmas has always been full of excitements ever since I can remember. At least a fortnight before the morning of the Nativity, the climax of all our preparations, we were decorating not only in the nursery, but throughout the house, for Mother loved to decorate. Will Stuart came into the house with armfuls of woodland decorations, and, balancing somewhat precariously on a step-ladder, put garlands round the antlers of Martindale red deer stags hanging in the hall, or upon the wide-faced Parliamentary clock, while Bill Slee, the under-gardener, carried in yet more holly, laurel and trails of ivy for the celebrations. The high-ceilinged kitchen with copper pans and jelly shapes was likewise decorated, and the Old Hall too, where a log fire blazed continuously within the medieval arch, providing constant welcome and friendship for all who came and went from the great outdoors.

A large Christmas tree usually stood in the drawing room or in the front hall with the legendary Star of the East twinkling from the highest pinnacle of the tree, while other decorations were brought out of the large dress box where they could be stored away safely. We children loved the decorations, particularly our favourite ornamental birds which glittered in the firelight. Mother played carols on the piano, or records on the wind-up His Master's Voice gramophone, while we sang the well-loved words together with the household until Father Christmas appeared with his sack of presents. Of course Will Stuart and his Jeannie came too; they lived in Deer Park cottage by the archway, and both were constant members of Dacre Church choir and of Cousin Dorothy Hasell's village choir, winners on several occasions of Cumberland's Rural Choirs Festival in Carlisle. Not only was he a singer, Will played the violin, playing for many a dance in surrounding villages. Someone who played the fiddle well was always in demand.

Church and carols were very much part of our Christmas; we all helped decorate Dacre Church; this ancient church was part of our lives; Cousin Dorothy always arranged the flowers in the altar vases throughout the year, while we assisted Mother wherever possible; the stone effigy of the Crusader, lying with crossed legs, was never forgotten by Grandfather; he laid a posy on the Crusader's prayerful hands, for this Lord Dacre had gone to fight for the Holy Land, and we as children were taught never to forget such acts of faithfulness and bravery.

There were other children, too, who must never be forgotten in our own happiness. Some of these lived in orphanages, having no complete home of their own. We always accompanied Mother, bearing toys to bring a little extra happiness to these children. Frequently the toys were things with which we really did not want to part. I remember a pair of fascinating musical stools made of gilded cane-work, and a very ancient gramophone whose records, made of a type of cardboard with squared holes for notes, played such tunes as "Bluebells of Scotland"; these would be antique treasures in present times.

Around New Year, a much-looked-forward-to dance took place in the big kitchen given by our parents for everyone who worked in the house or on the estate, and for their friends. The kitchen floor, shiny red composition laid on top of medieval flag-stones, made an excellent floor for dancing especially when a packet of Lux had been scattered on its surface to make it more slippery than usual. Joe Hall from Penruddock played hilarious music on his piano-accordion which he played extremely well. Joe played for many local dances and was a popular musician. The Lancers was a favourite dance in which the girls were frequently whirled off their feet in the hilarity of the moment; the Military Twostep was another. A marvellous supper was laid out in the Old Hall, and in the intervals Will and Jeannie enter-tained the assembled company with songs, and so did anyone else who felt like doing so. Father fancied he was quite a songster and always played his part. Mother recited with dramatic feeling; sometimes "The Boy who won the Victoria Cross". The Armistice of 1918 was not long past and very clear in the memories of all those present.

Meanwhile, my sister Margaret and I were supposed to be fast asleep in the night nursery, directly above the kitchen, and to small children the noise and the music seemed interminable. It was impossible to go to sleep.

Out in the garden in sheltered corners, flowers were already proclaiming this sea-son of joy and festivity. Christmas roses never failed to bloom, for Will was a dedicated plantsman. Tucked up with leafmould on the north side of a holly hedge, the snow white flowers, like roses borne on naked stems, emerged from clusters of deeply incisored evergreen leaves, sometimes tinged with pink externally, and emi-nently suitable for growing in the shelter of shrubs, but revelling in a generous coating of leafmould. Christmas Roses always decorated the candlelit dinner table, but sometimes aconites also arrived in time to make merry for this wonderful festi-val, their shining golden faces emerging joyfully beneath the shelter of lilac trees to join in animation with the children on this special occasion.

When we were old enough to have ponies and an elderly donkey, our first thoughts before opening presents was to give them a good feed, so that they should not feel forgotten. The fallow deer in the park were our friends too, some even eat-ing out of our hands; they were always glad of an extra bite.

Carols were sung without fail in Dacre's venerable church, after which cousins and old friends came to tea or to a candlelit dinner. Then we all played hide-and-seek all over the house, when cousin Eva Hasell, who was great fun and quite rotund, frequently got stuck hiding beneath low fourposter beds! Mother was a romantic, bringing us up to enjoy candlelight and its effects. There always seemed to be stars shining in the mysterious deep blue dome of Heaven on Christmas night when I was a child. Were those twinkling stars leading us on into the unknown? One could only gaze into the night sky in wonder, at the incomprehensible.

LITTLE BROWN DONKEY'S TALE

The evening was dark and wintry
As we played on the kitchen floor;
Just as we tidied for bedtime
Came a strange, hard knock on the door.

The children peeped past the curtain
As I cautiously looked out to see;
'Twas an old brown donkey, determined
To enter and settle for tea.

He urgently wanted to tell us
Of the wonderful baby, newborn —
Not born with the comforts of homelife,
But a stable, remote and forlorn.

There was sweet smelling hay for his cradle
And kind cattle to soothe him to sleep;
While a little brown donkey breathed softly
And small stable mice came to peep.

The baby, this most wonderful baby
With such beautiful pale blue eyes,
His face like a peach from an orchard
And tiny soft hands — lest he cries . . .

His mother, so young and so fragile
Held her baby right close to her breast
And gazed at her babe with enrapture
To be sure she would give him her best.

Dear Joseph watched closely beside them
This first born, and God given son;
He gave them his heart in endeavour
To care true for this small Holy One.

For the angels ascertained his Mary
Of their babe that would set the world free;
But these first coming years of his childhood
Must be carefree and happy, with me.

This sweet mother cradled her loved one
While good Joseph's arms cradled the two
And angels sang songs in the starlight
For the babe born especially for you.

Our children gazed in a dreamworld
Their faces were radiant and shone;
The fire burned up bright, on this strange starlit night
And the little brown donkey was gone.

October 1988

149

EPILOGUE

There is no end and no readily defined beginning to the seasons in the amazingly wonderful world of plants. While they rest, they are already preparing themselves for the slow but certain resurgence of new life, which from days unnumbered has been called Spring.

Flowers come and go the whole year round; there is never a month without a flower in bloom, whether it be a daisy growing in a lawn . . . still there as they grew when we ourselves were small, and as years pass our grandchildren make daisy-chains from these same little flowers. Or, be it a rose, peeping into a frost-patterned window, as our fragrant 'Old Blush China' roses have done so many years; or jasmine, brilliant golden starlike flowers on many a winter's day.

Gardens have scarcely been tucked up and laid to rest; new trees planted during these dormant weeks; leaves gathered into clamps; manure spread, ready to sink and feed with winter's snow and rain, before seemingly long weeks of winter have flown past and it is already time to write fresh clean labels and sow seeds. Spring's earlier morning lights waken us, almost unexpectedly. It is the hidden hour to rise from a world of sleep, just as trees and plants in the countryside around us are most certainly wakening too. Primroses, daffodils, wood anemones and tiny woodsorrel, their fragile white bells streaked with grey, growing in family gatherings within cosy beech woods. Celandines, glowing with sunshine that becomes stronger as day follows day in the race to be in time . . . for what? . . . to grow, to bloom, to set seed which will ripen and be scattered in order to create yet another generation, each after its own kind.

Nothing ever dies: every plant particle has its necessary use; its old dress clothes and feeds. Winter is the necessary period of rest for all things which we human beings also require before Spring, of a surety, will return. For the Lord of winter's glorious Sunsets, is also the Lord of the Sunrise.